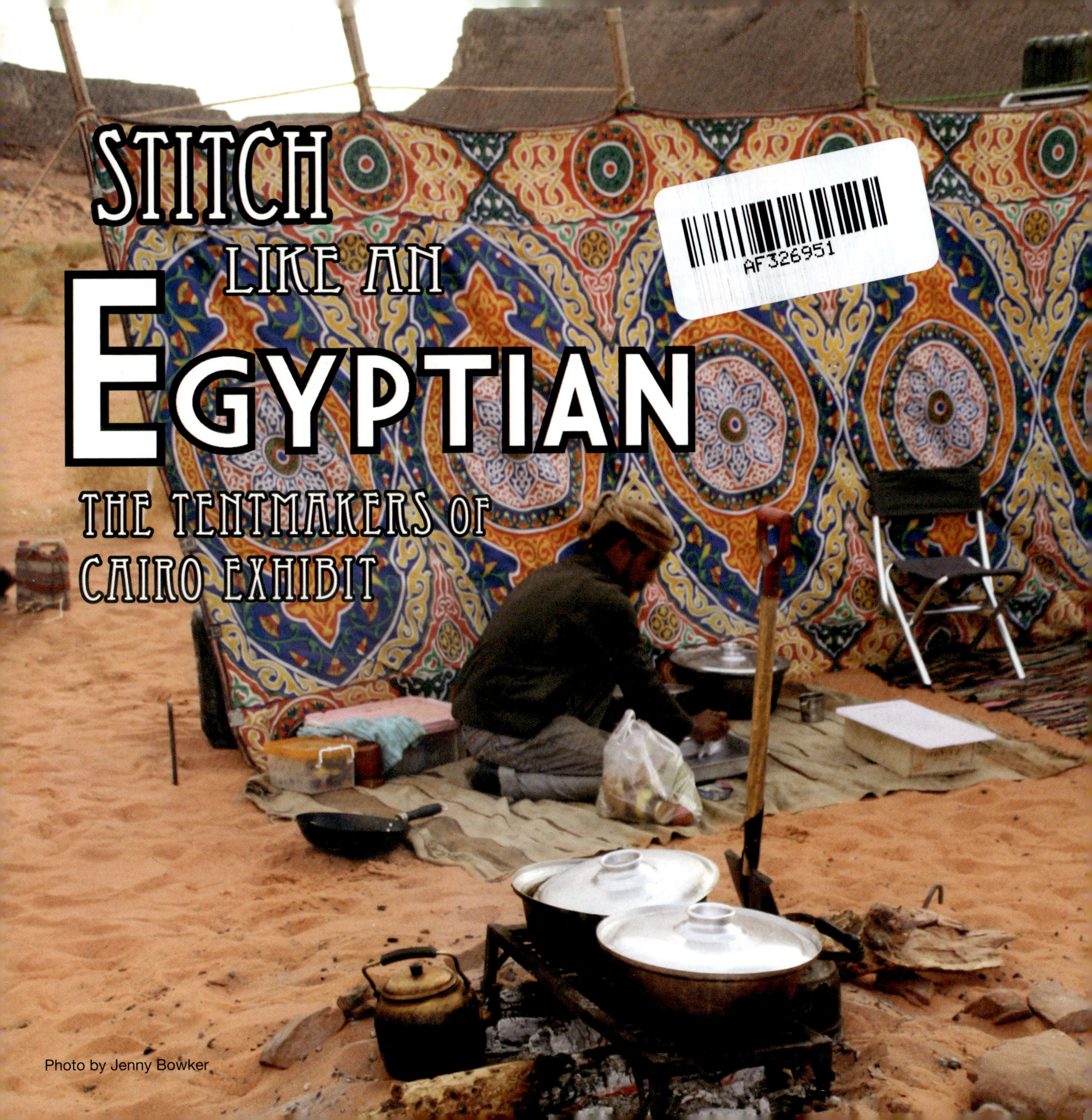

STITCH
LIKE AN
EGYPTIAN
THE TENTMAKERS OF
CAIRO EXHIBIT
Photo by Jenny Bowker

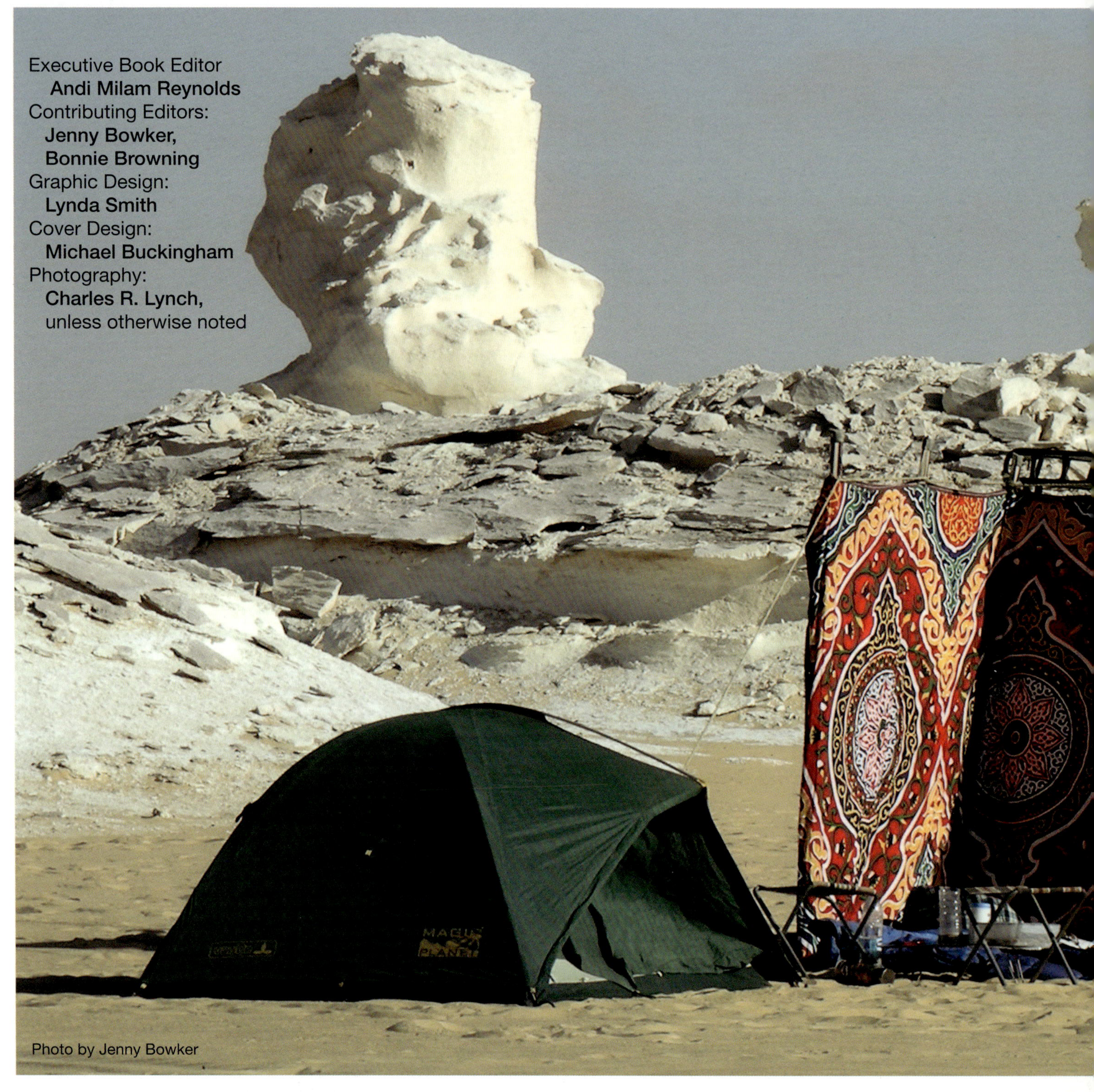

Executive Book Editor
Andi Milam Reynolds
Contributing Editors:
Jenny Bowker,
Bonnie Browning
Graphic Design:
Lynda Smith
Cover Design:
Michael Buckingham
Photography:
Charles R. Lynch,
unless otherwise noted

Photo by Jenny Bowker

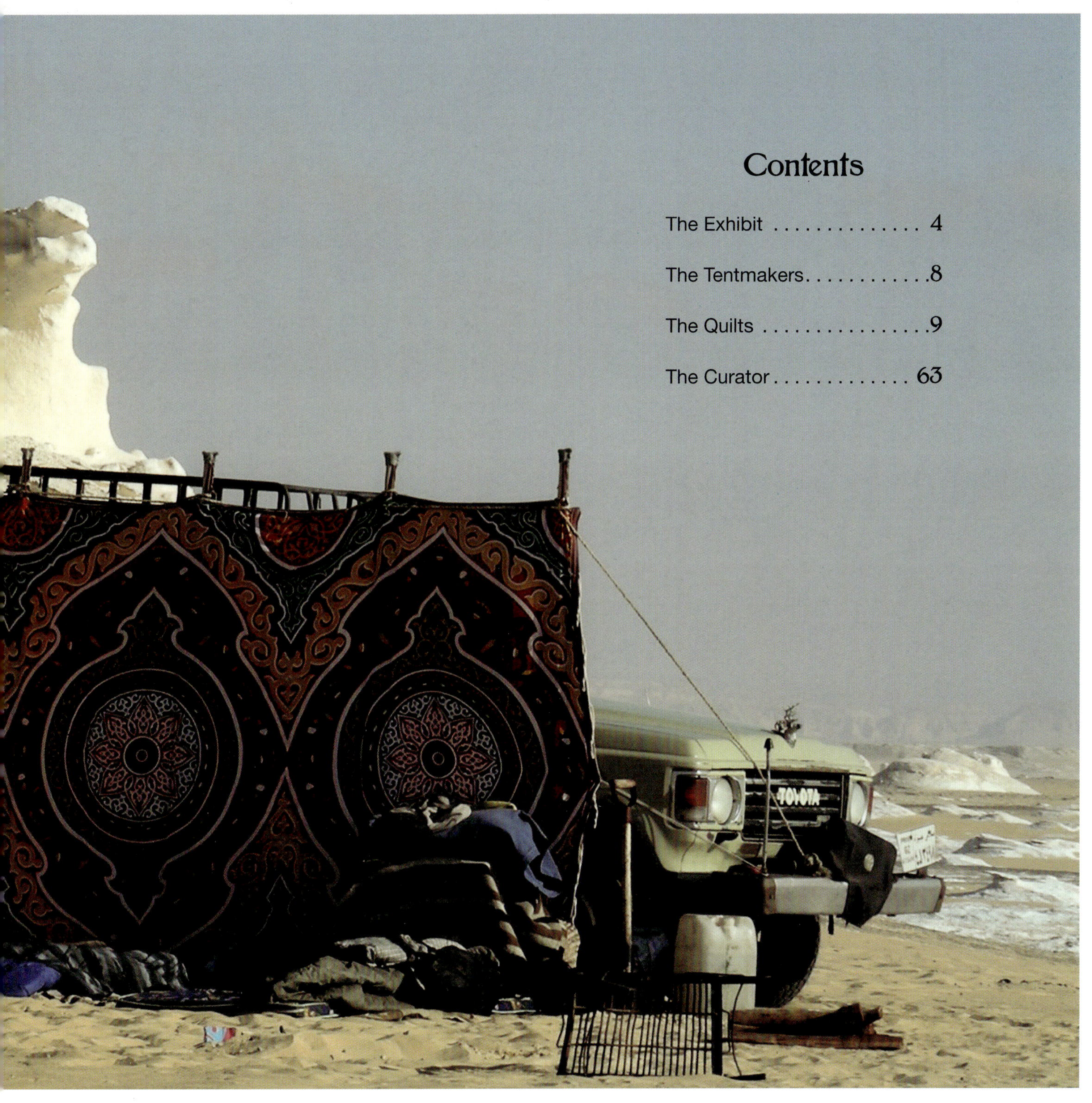

Contents

The Exhibit

by Bonnie Browning, Executive Show Director

Quilts are featured at the four premiere shows produced by the American Quilter's Society to recognize the artistry of today's quiltmakers. In addition to the contest quilts that compete for $250,000 in cash awards per year, each show also includes several special quilt exhibits, ranging from those displaying new and antique quilts from across the U.S. to international exhibits.

After reading and viewing information about the Tentmakers of Cairo exhibit at the Birmingham, England, show, I set out to see if we could exhibit these quilts at one of our AQS Quilt Shows. I discovered that Jenny Bowker, quilt and textile artist and wife of the former Australian ambassador to Egypt, had worked with the Tentmakers to exhibit their work in England. She had met them while she lived in Egypt. We began a three-continent collaboration to make the arrangements for Stitch Like an Egyptian: The Tentmakers of Cairo to debut at the AQS Quilt Show in Grand Rapids, Michigan, August 22-25, 2012. This would be the first time the Tentmakers of Cairo have had their quilts displayed in the United States.

Jenny made a trip from Australia to Egypt in March 2012 to hand select the quilts. Some may call their work tapestries, but they are not woven like a tapestry. These artists use a soft, thick cotton background to sew into and over. Then you'll see two or three layers of appliqué; no batting or filler is used for these pieces. The backing may be plain canvas or the canvas may be covered with a layer of fabric. Because they were intended to be parts of tents, the pieces are heavy. At our request, each piece has a hanging sleeve. While they may not be quilts that are stitched together with quilting stitches like we are accustomed to, people are amazed at the detail and quality of the appliqué in their work.

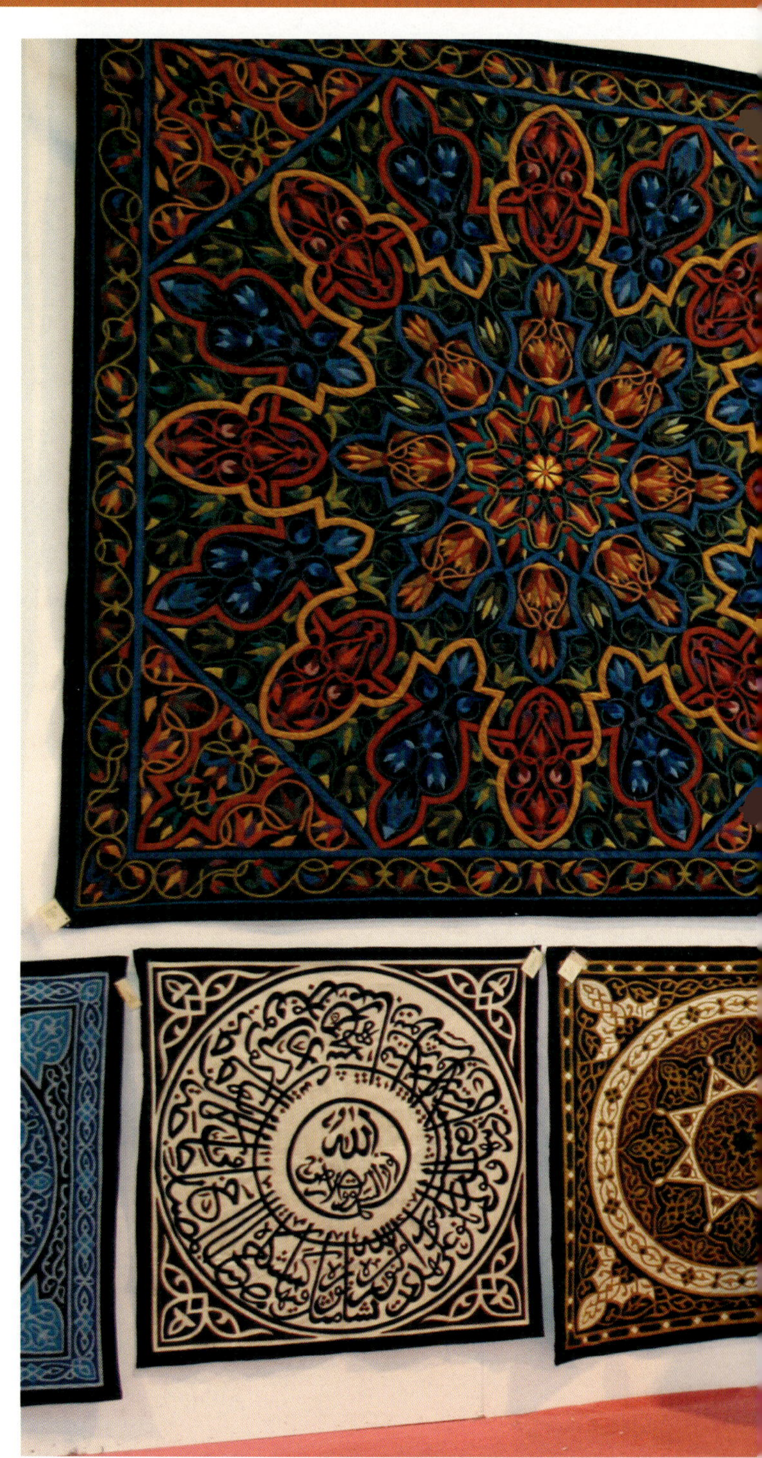

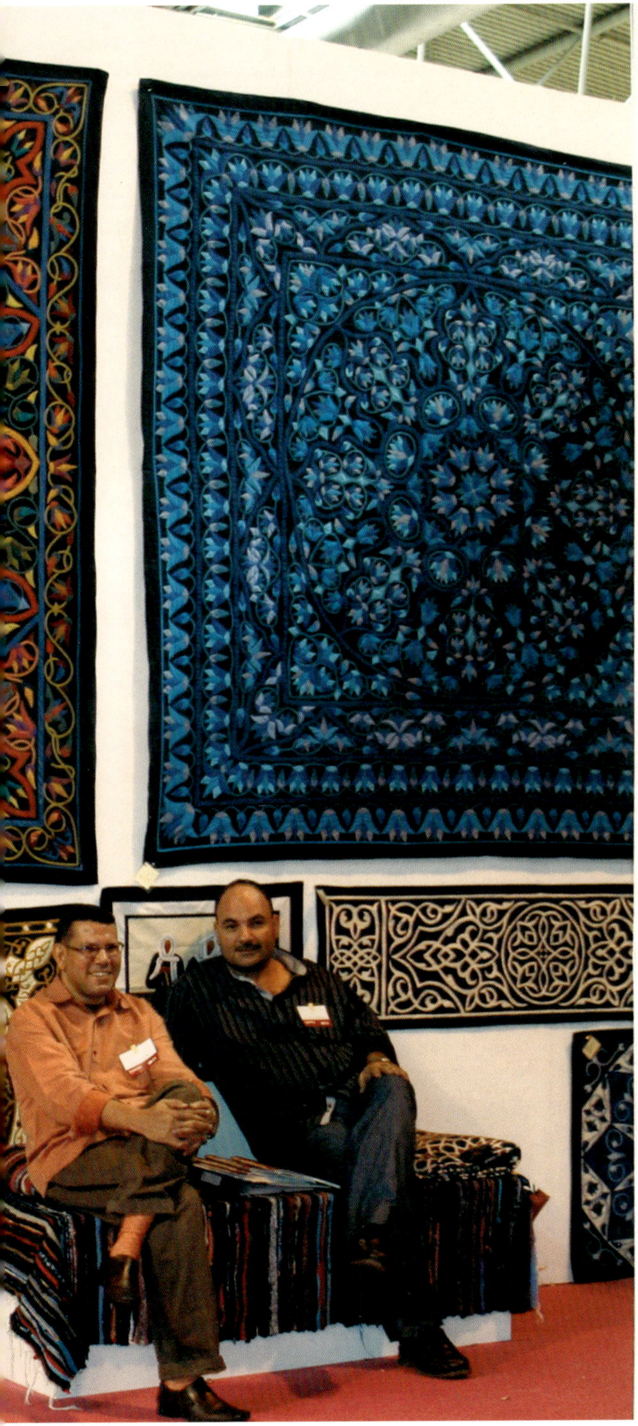

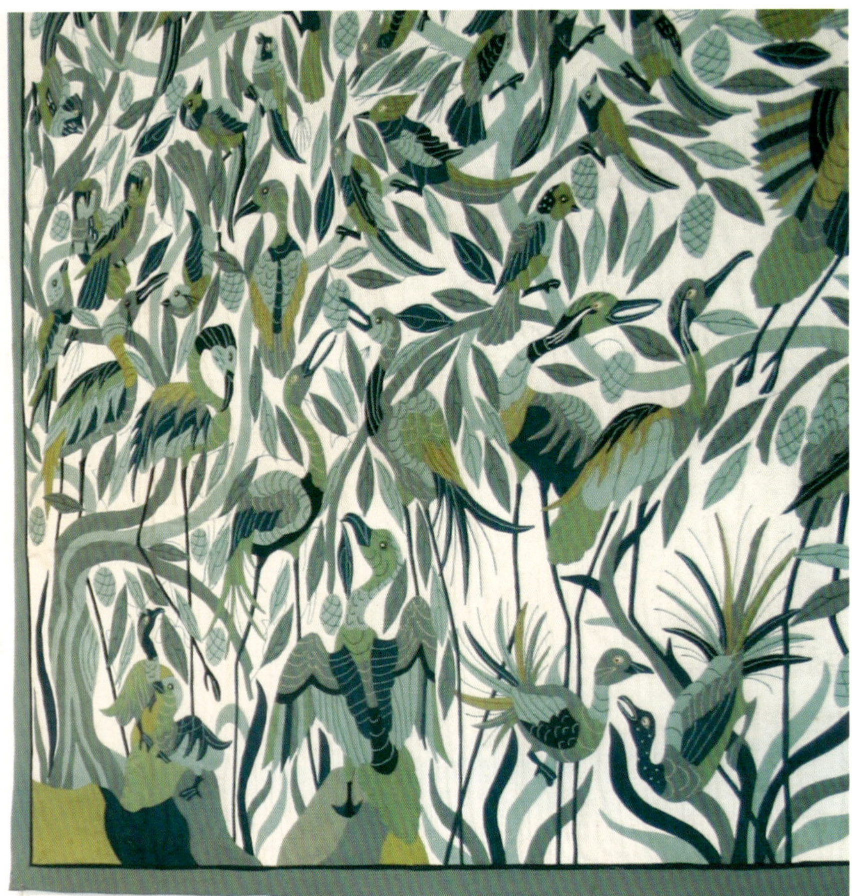

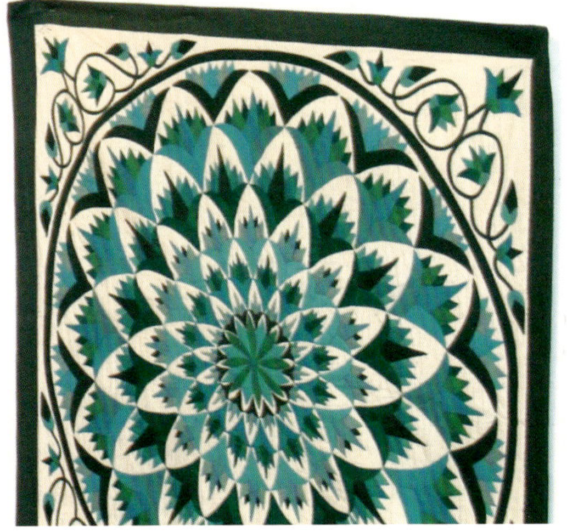

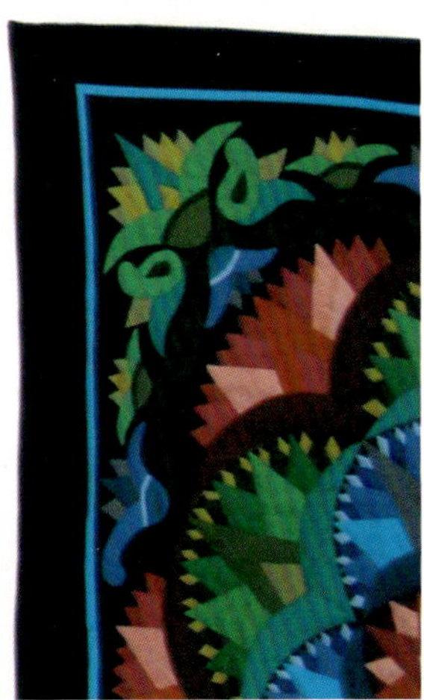

Because of the large number of pieces in this exhibit—95—it was determined that it would be easier for AQS to import the quilts for display at several of our shows; and, they could be sold so quilters and quilt collectors in this country could add samples of the Tentmakers' work to their collections. When the quilts arrived at the AQS office in May, they were immediately photographed to create this exhibit catalogue.

To enhance the exhibit, what better than to have some Tentmakers demonstrate their craft? AQS issued a letter of invitation to two of the men—Hosam Hanafy Ahmed Mahmoud and Tarek Abdelhay Hafez Abouelenin. A call to Kentucky Senator Mitch McConnell's office gave us information on the materials that would be needed for these men to request a visa to come to the U.S. They then had to schedule an appointment with the U.S. Embassy visa office in Cairo. All of their paperwork was in order and their visas were issued to attend.

Altogether, it took more than half a year of planning, communicating, and sewing to secure the 95 pieces in this first-ever U.S. exhibit of Stitch Like an Egyptian: The Tentmakers of Cairo Exhibit.

The American Quilter's Society is pleased to continue providing unparalleled quilt show experiences, contests, and exhibits.

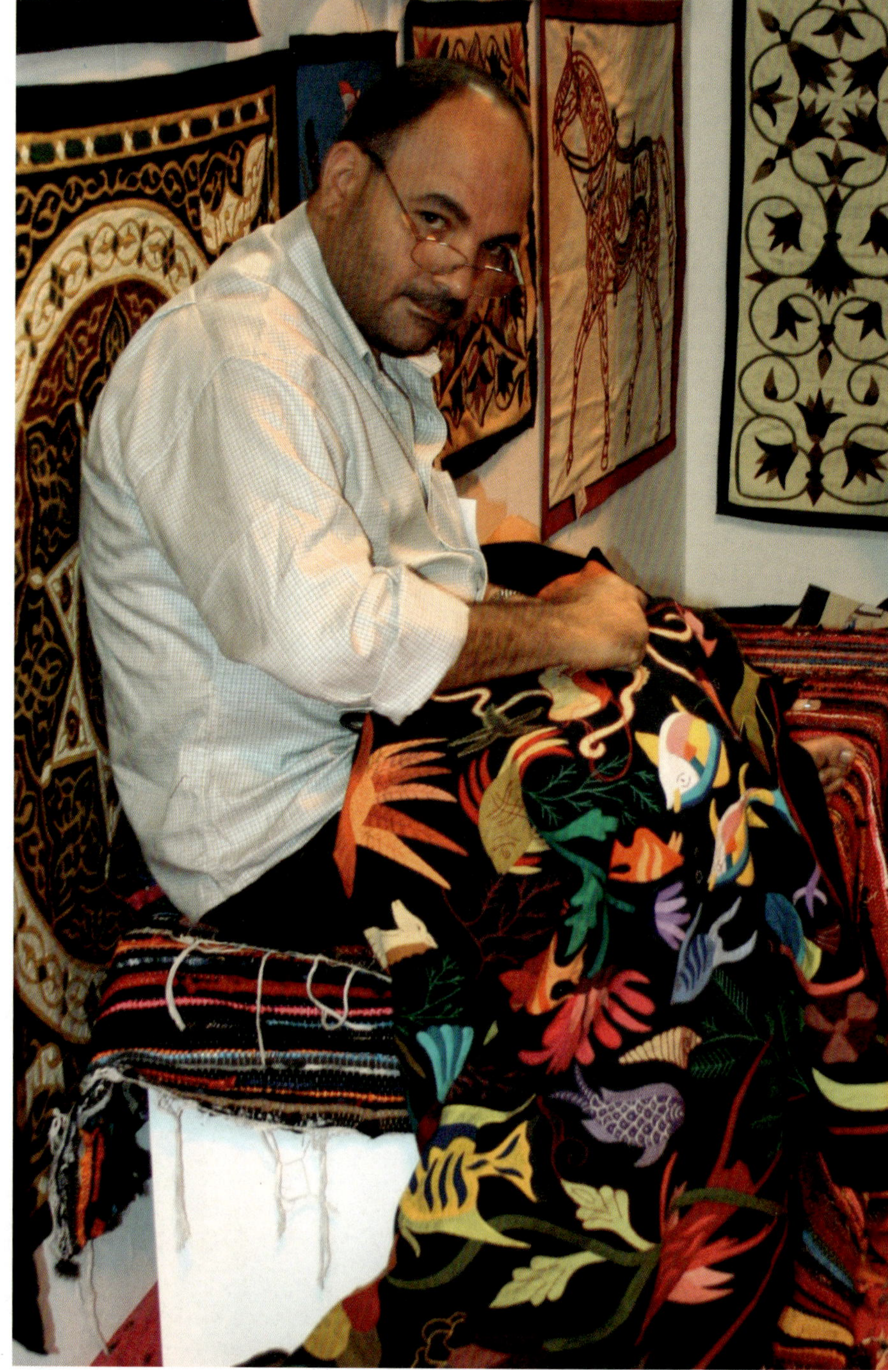

Tarek Abouelenin

Photo by Jenny Bowker

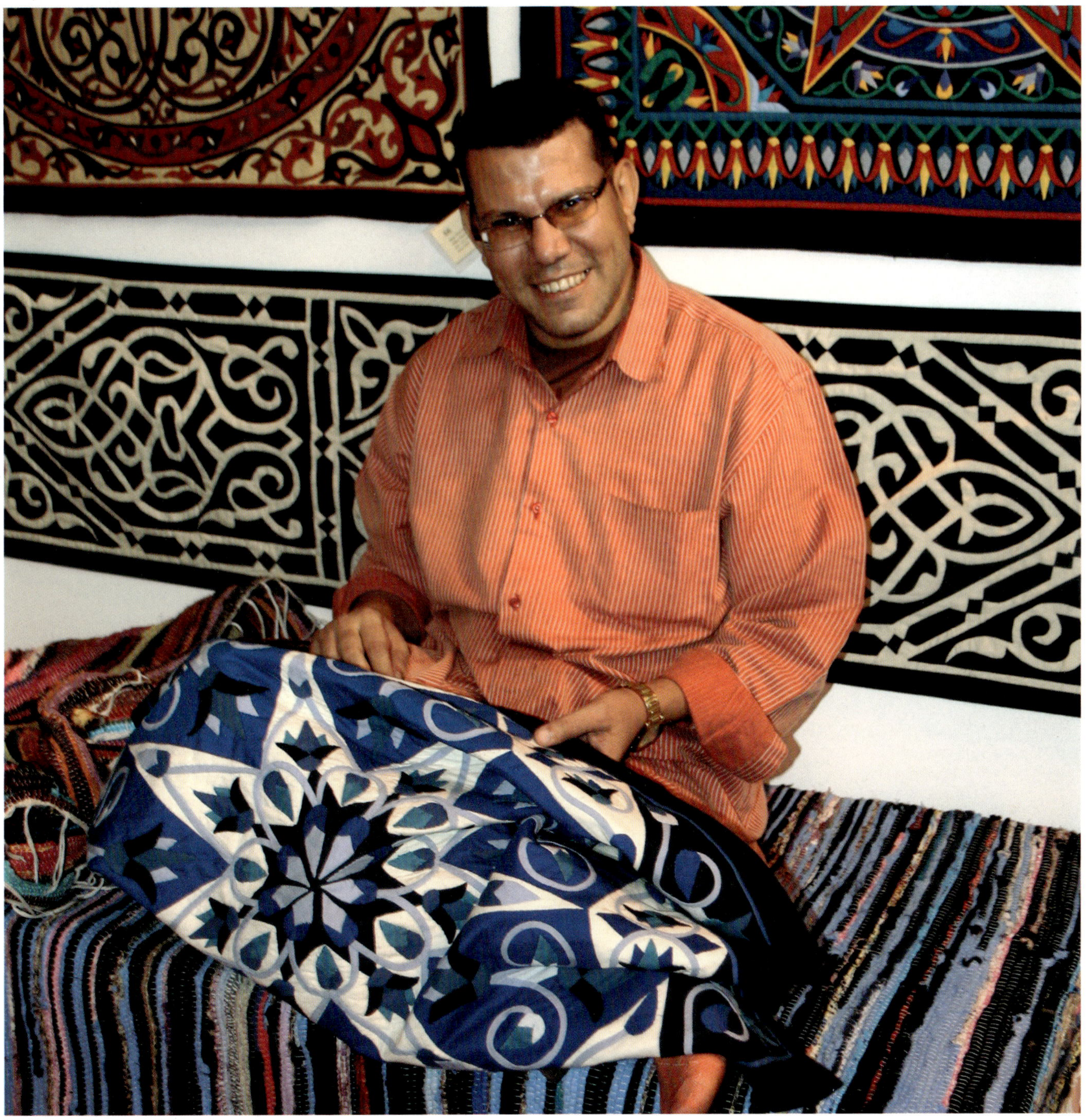

Hosam Mahmoud

The Tentmakers
by Jenny Bowker, Exhibit Curator

The American Quilter's Society brings the appliqué artistry of the tentmakers of Cairo, Egypt, to the U.S. for the first time ever! The exhibit was curated by Jenny Bowker, international textile artist and wife of a former Australian ambassador to Egypt. She has been helping to make the world aware of the beautiful work of the 45 master tentmakers and their stitchers who continue to ply their trade.

Jenny has helped the men exhibit their work in Australia, England, Spain, France, and now, for the first time in the United States, at the AQS Quilt Show at the DeVos Place Convention Center, Grand Rapids, Michigan, August 22 - 25, 2012. Two of the tentmakers, Hosam Hanafy Ahmed Mahmoud and Tarek Abdelhay Hafez Abouelenin, have been invited to attend the show to demonstrate their method of appliqué. Their designs are complex radiating patterns or are inspired by medieval Mosque floors or door decorations, wall panels in Pharaonic tombs, or Koranic calligraphy.

The artists are from Khan Khayamiya—the Market of the Tentmakers, which stretches opposite Bab Zuweilah in the heart of Old Islamic Cairo. This is the only remaining place in Old Cairo that still has a covering over the street. The sun slants in dusty fingers through the openings in the roof. An occasional donkey cart or truck forces its way through, and good-natured people step aside to make room in the narrow street. Brightly colored hangings cover the walls and hang outside the doors, and stitchers sit and sew in every shop.

Tentmaker work is brilliantly colored appliqué, and it is usually men who make it. The name comes from the fact that their work used to line tents or screens covered in appliqué that could decorate a whole street, or define an area for a Ramadan dinner table, a wedding, a henna party, or a funeral. It was never intended to be fine and beautiful work, but served to create drama and color. Like many native or folk arts, these appliqué pieces are not highly valued in Egypt; they are considered utilitarian, made by laborers, and even unlucky because of the association with funerals. The current trend is to use preprinted imitation synthetic panels instead of handmade pieces.

Fortunately, today's quiltmakers recognize the skill needed by the tentmakers to make their beautiful and colorful appliqués. A thriving international demand for their work keeps the few remaining tentmaker shops in business.

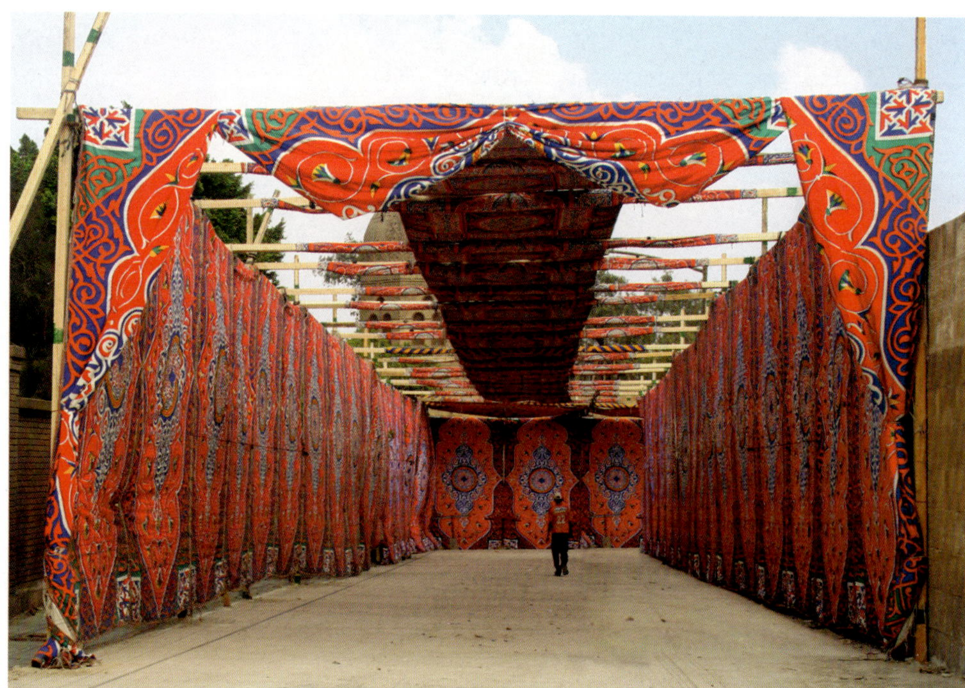

Photo by Jenny Bowker

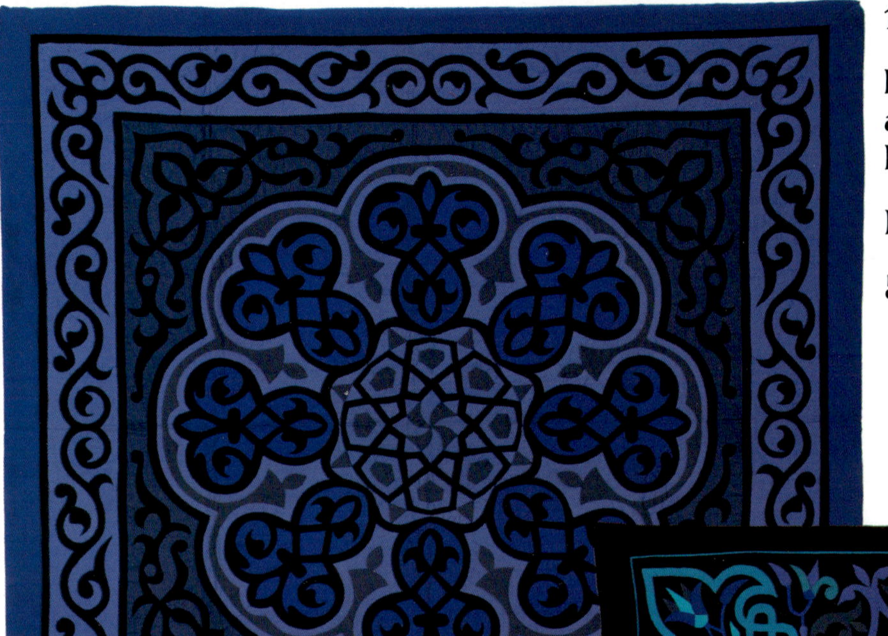

1 Amr Hassan

Islamic Design, geometric and fluid, central Eight-Point Star

Blues and blue-gray

51" x 51"

2 Amr Hassan

Islamic design of twisting and weaving lines, Romy elements

Blues and turquoise on navy

48" x 48"

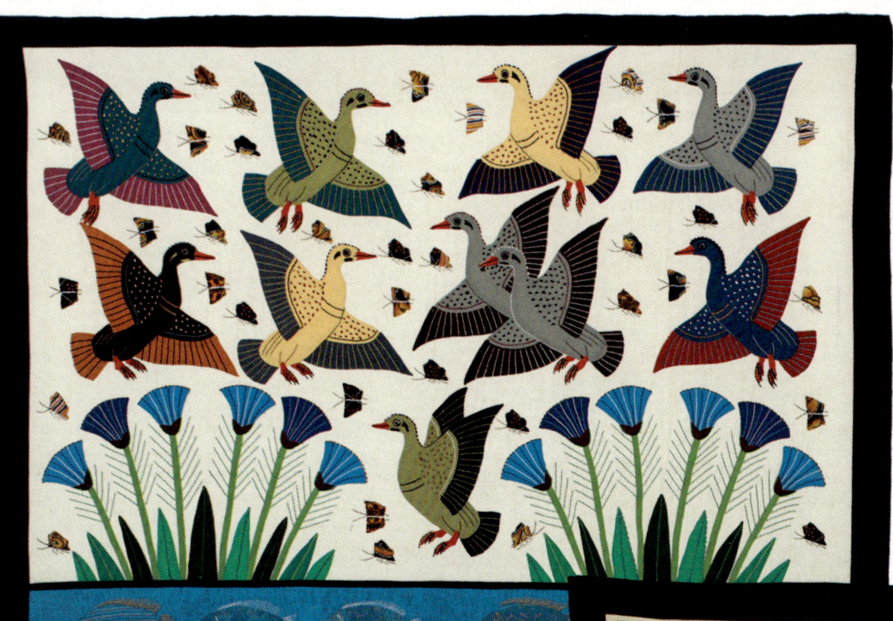

3 Amr Hassan, stitched by Mohamed Dendon

Paired ducks in flight with papyrus – tomb image

Navy borders, blue and multicolors on cream

45" x 35"

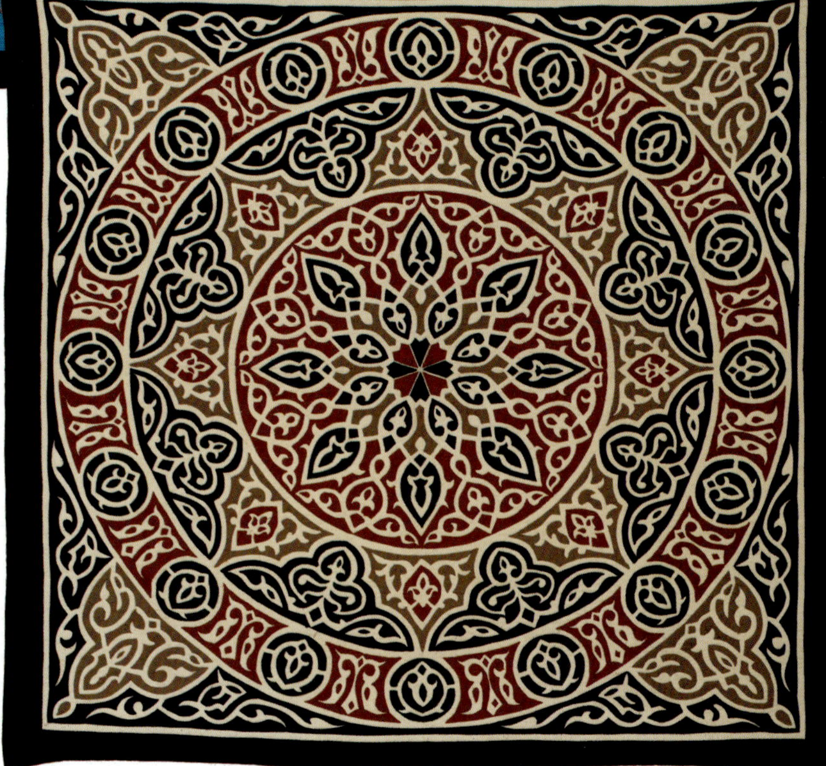

4 Sayed Aziz

Traditional Islamic design

Zippered Floor Pillow Cover

Navy border, beige, navy, terracotta, and cream

47" x 47"

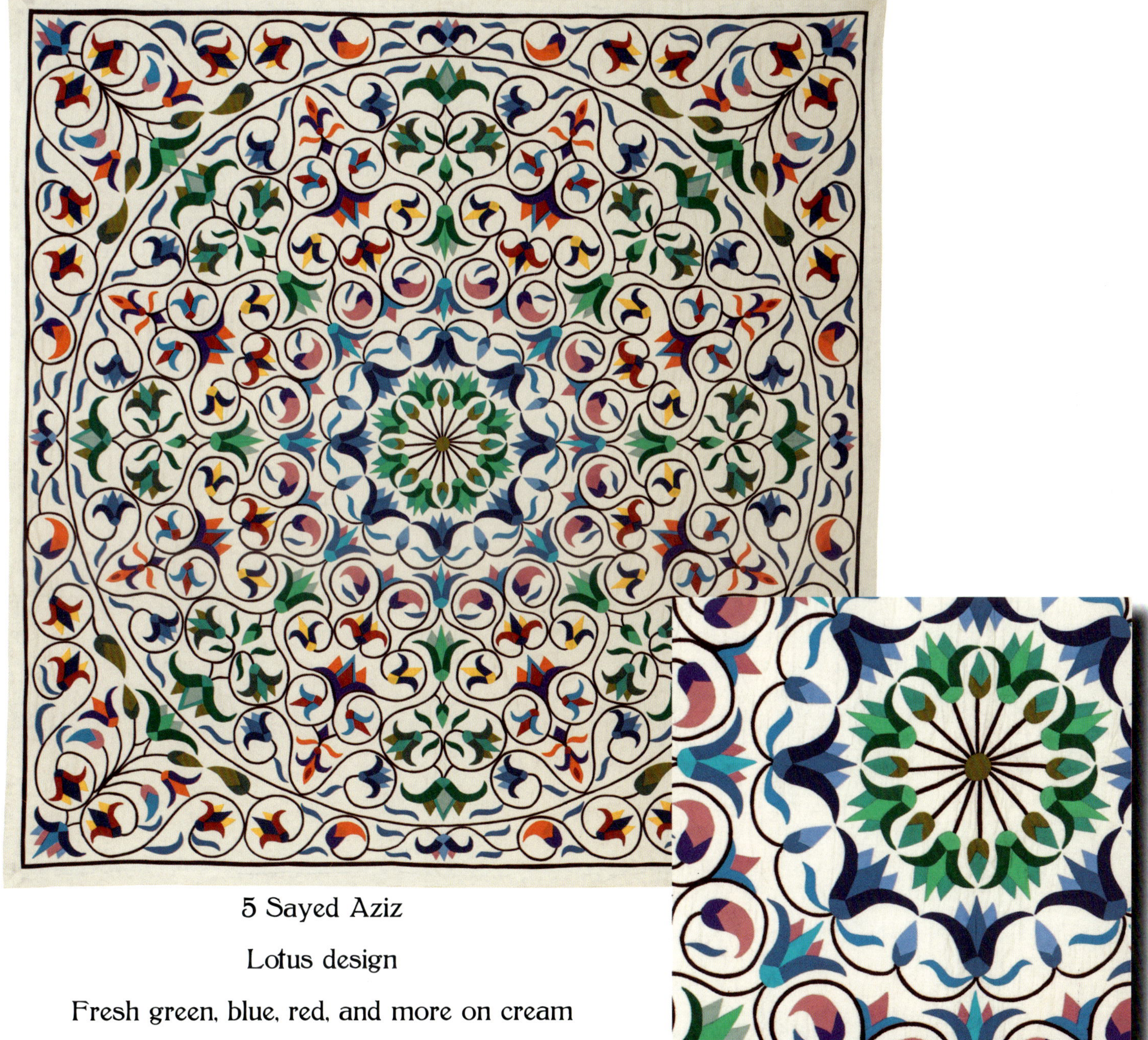

5 Sayed Aziz

Lotus design

Fresh green, blue, red, and more on cream

87" x 87"

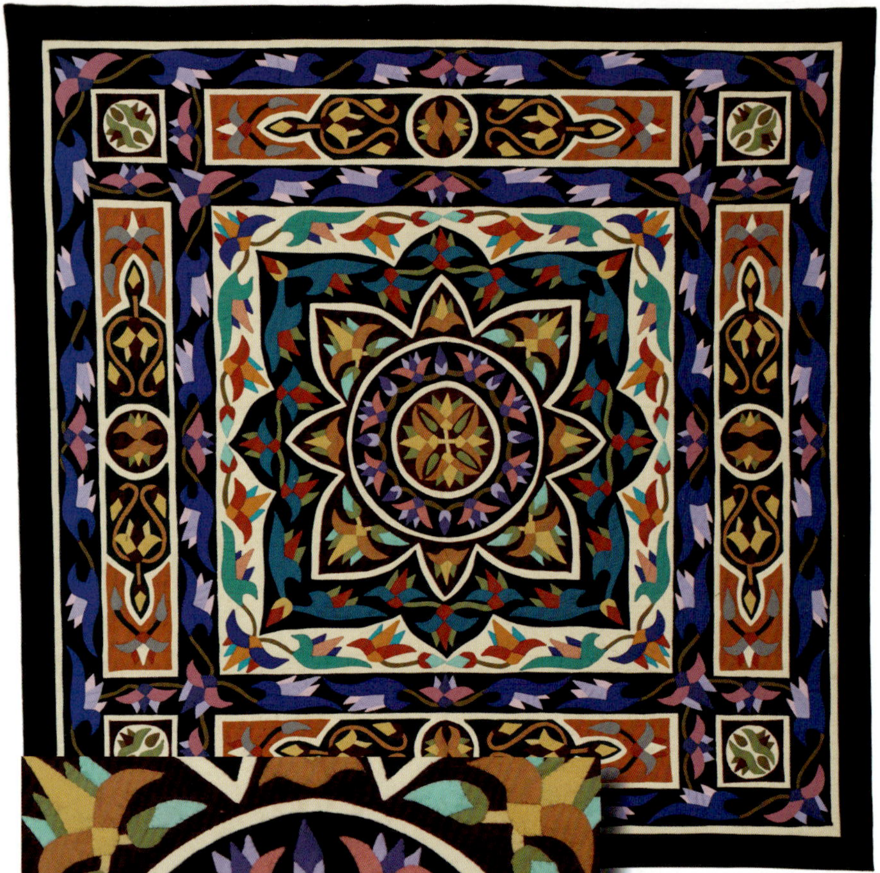

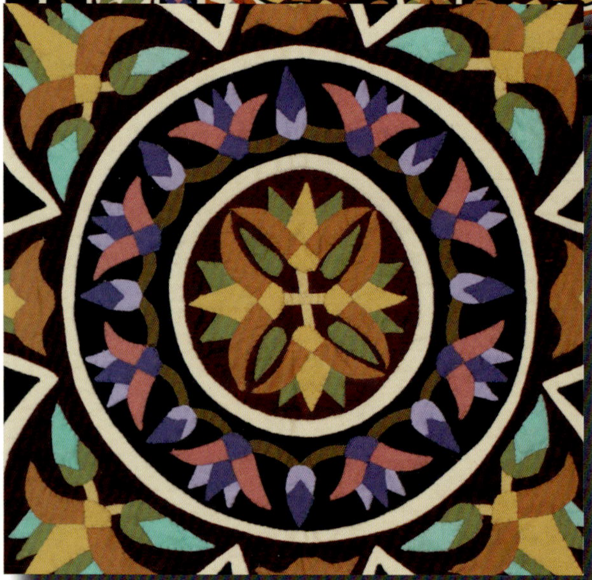

6 Sayed Aziz

Eight-fold Lotus design

Cream background with blue and terracotta borders, Lotus in many colors

47" x 47"

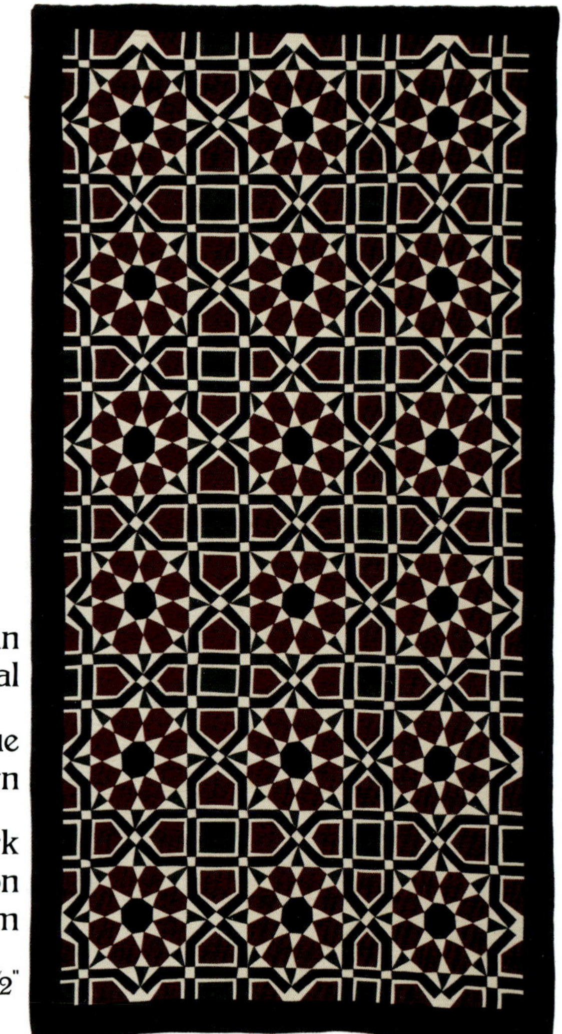

7 Hassan Kamal

Arabesque Design

Burgundy, dark green, navy on cream

71" x 35½"

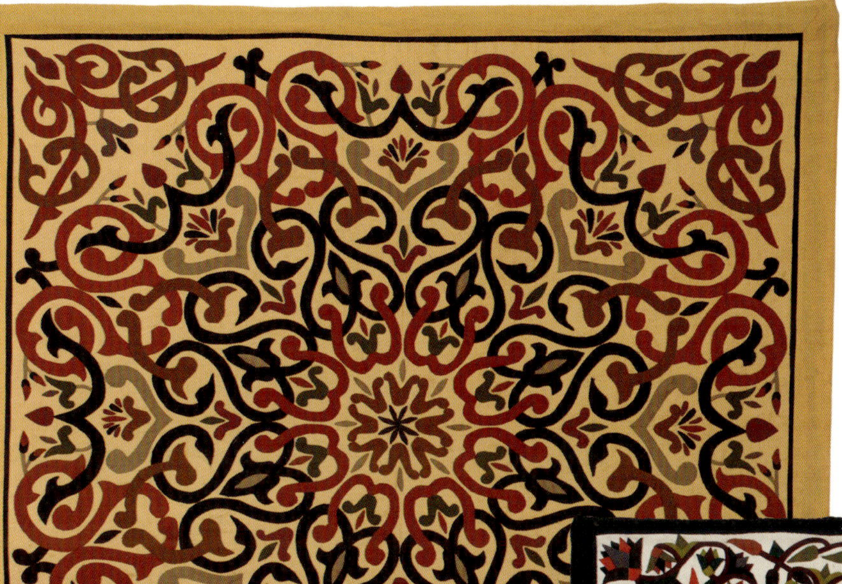

8 Hassan Kamal

Romy Design

Honey background
with red, tan, brown,
and beige

55" x 55"

9 Hassan Kamal

16–fold Design with Lotus

Greens, reds, on cream,
blue border

47" x 47"

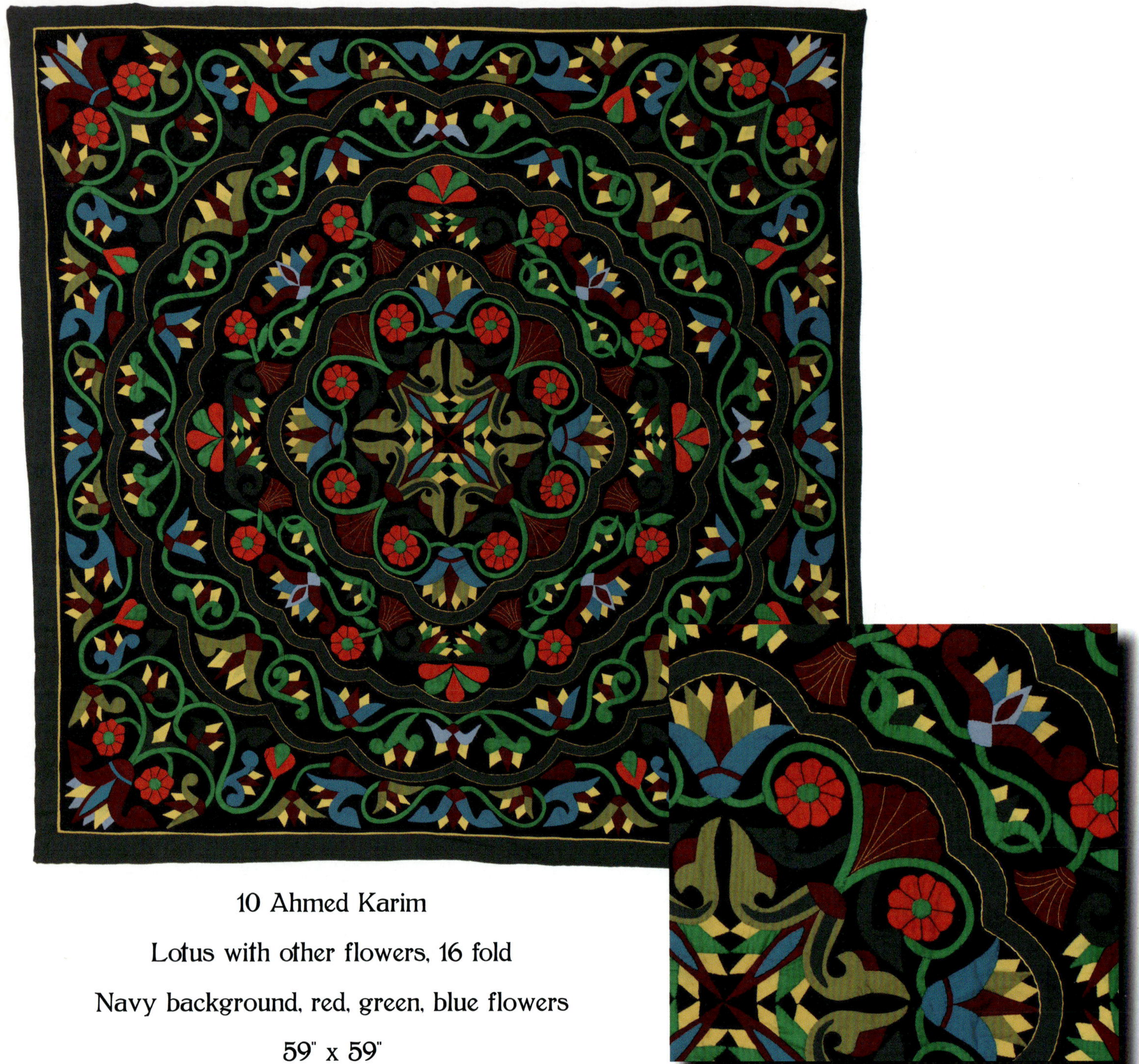

10 Ahmed Karim

Lotus with other flowers, 16 fold

Navy background, red, green, blue flowers

59" x 59"

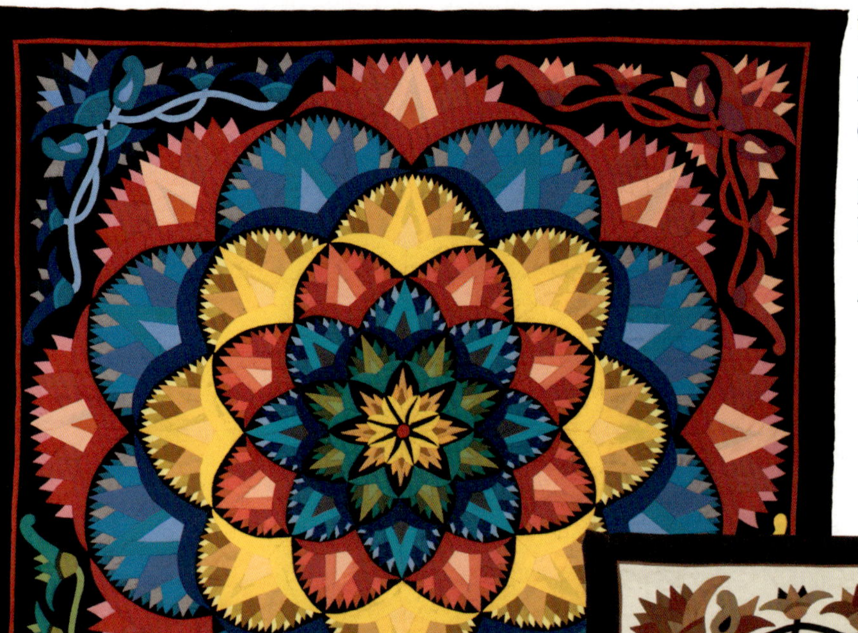

11 Ahmed Karim

Rainbow radiating Lotus design, 16 fold

Bright rainbow colors on black, corners different

47" x 47"

12 Ahmed Karim

Radiating Lotus Design, 16 fold

Browns and black on cream

47" x 47"

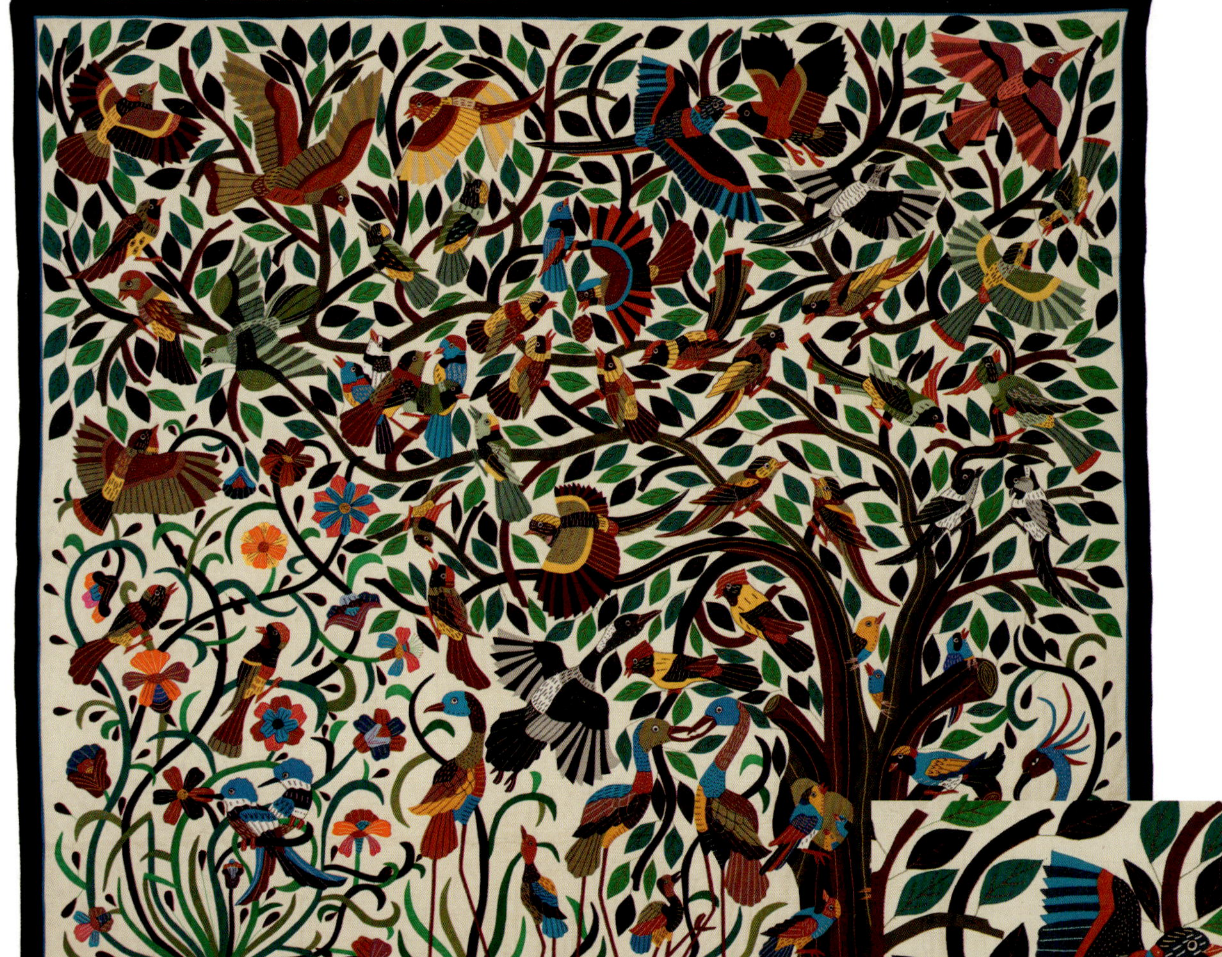

13 Ahmed Karim

Big Tree of Life – tomb image

Light background, multicolored birds and green leaves

98" x 98"

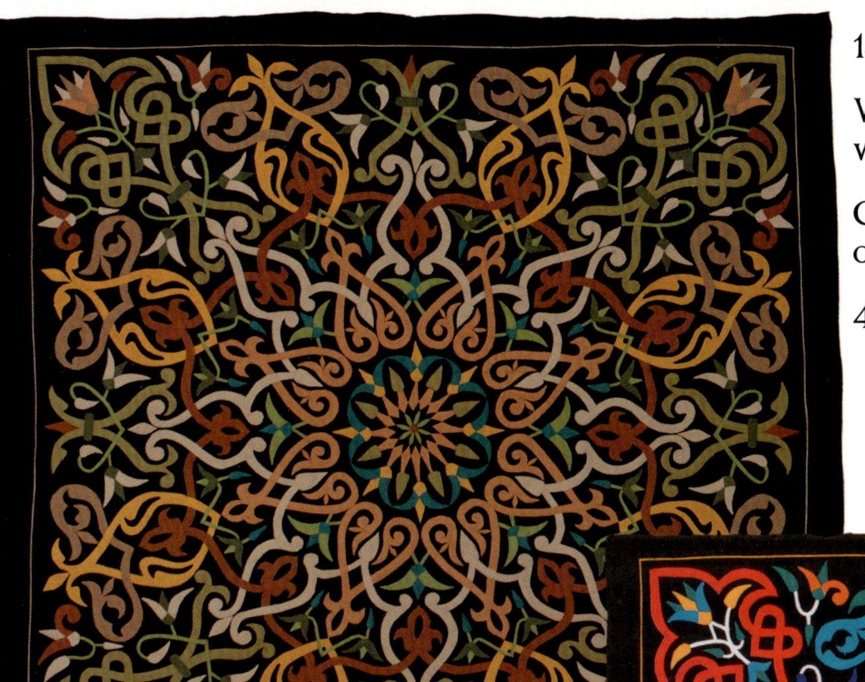

14 Mohamed Dendon

Woven Islamic design
with Romy and Lotus

Greens, beige, gold
on black

47" x 47"

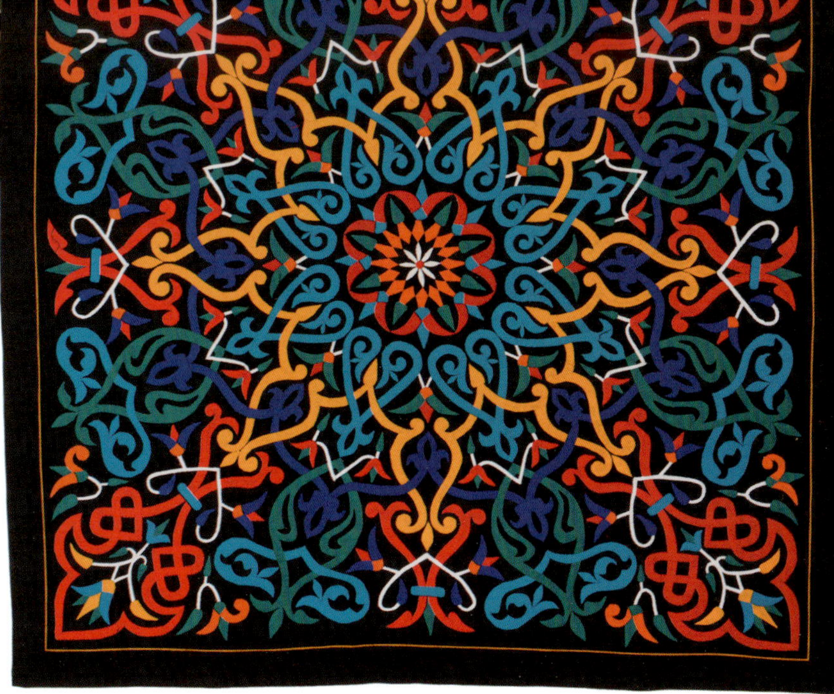

15 Mohamed Dendon

Woven Islamic design
with Romy and Lotus

Greens, beige, gold
on black

47" x 47"

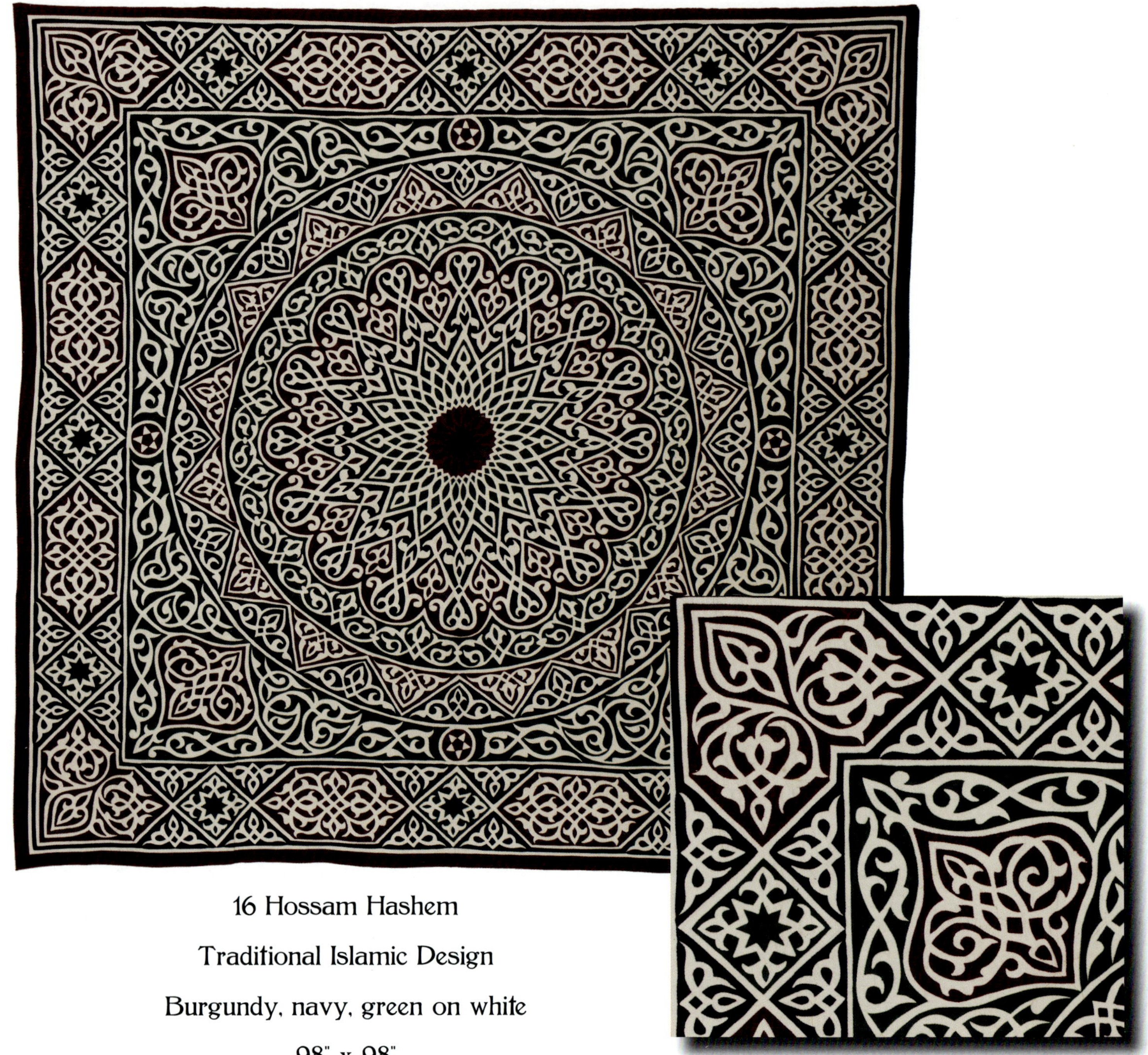

16 Hossam Hashem

Traditional Islamic Design

Burgundy, navy, green on white

98" x 98"

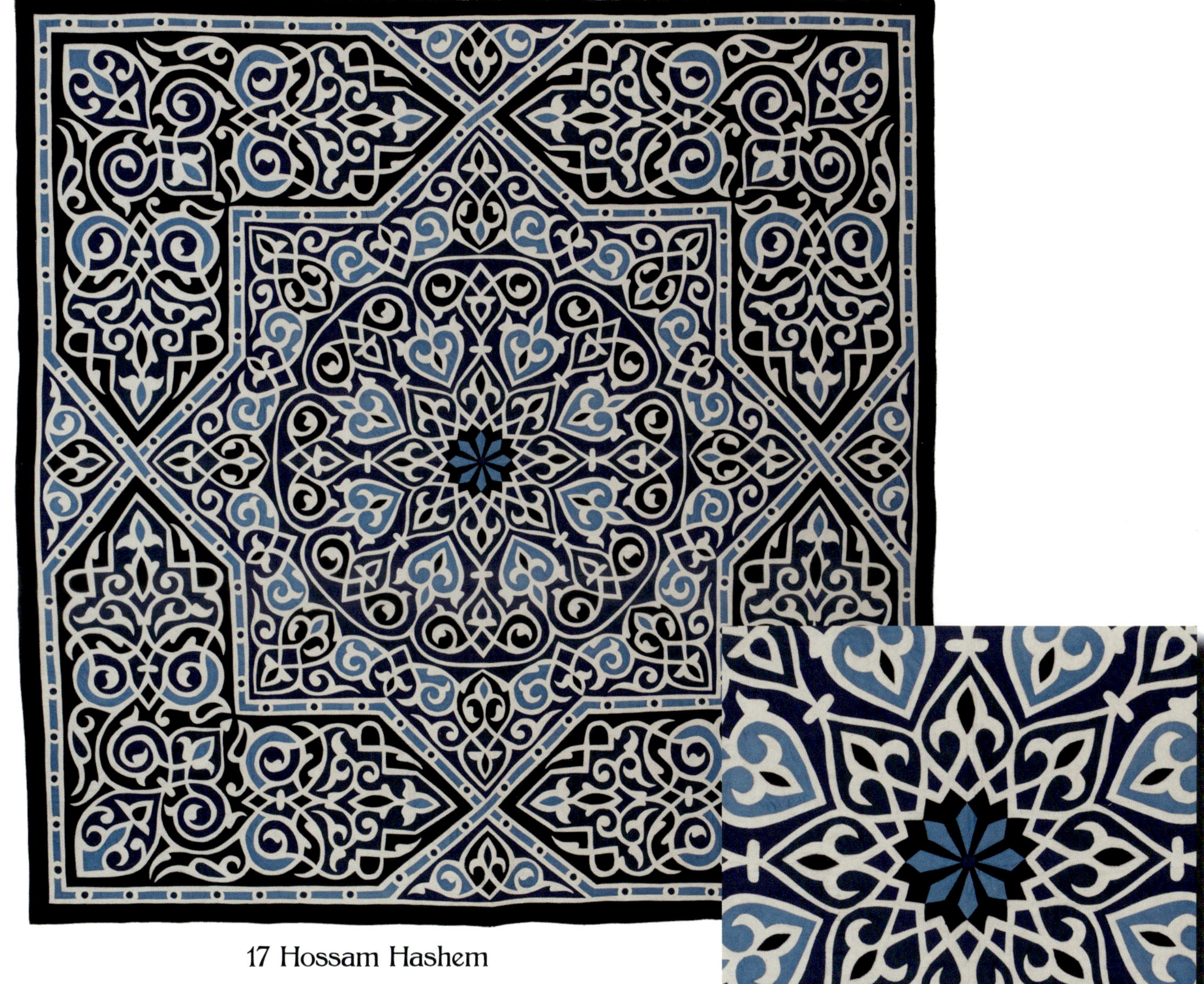

17 Hossam Hashem

Traditional Islamic Design

Blues on white, navy border

98" x 98"

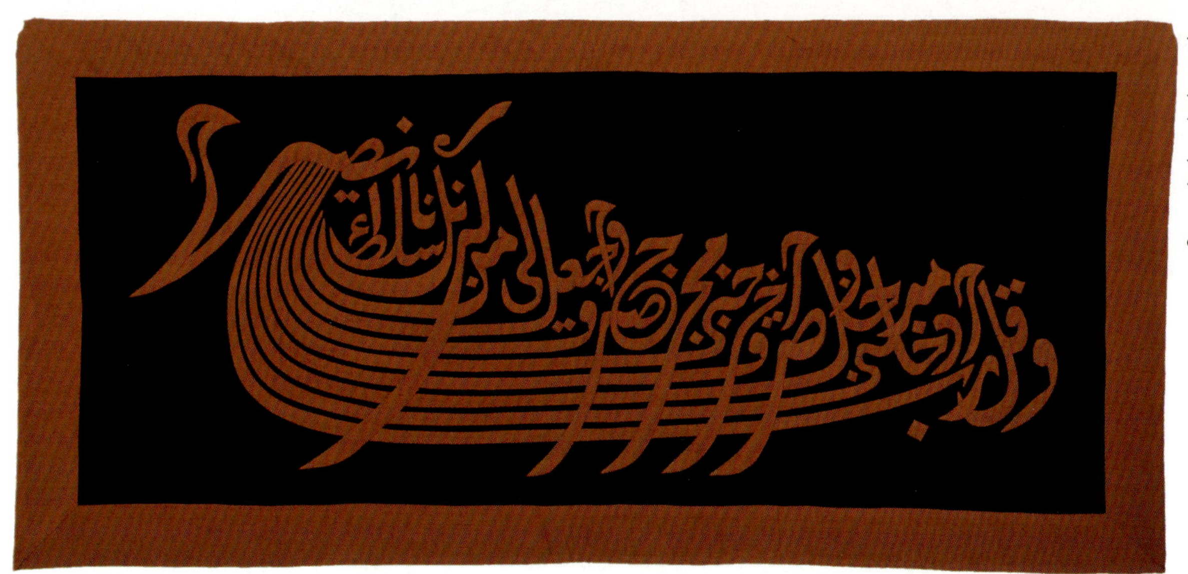

18 Ashraf Hashem

Boat calligraphy

Brown on black

39" x 20"

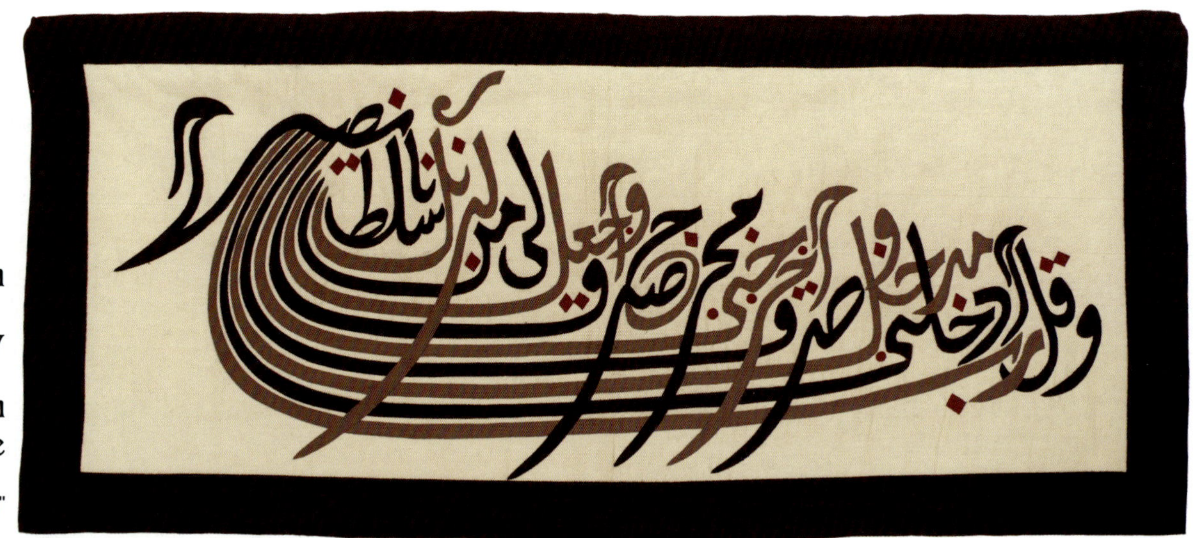

19 Ashraf Hashem

Boat Calligraphy

Brown and red on white

39" x 20"

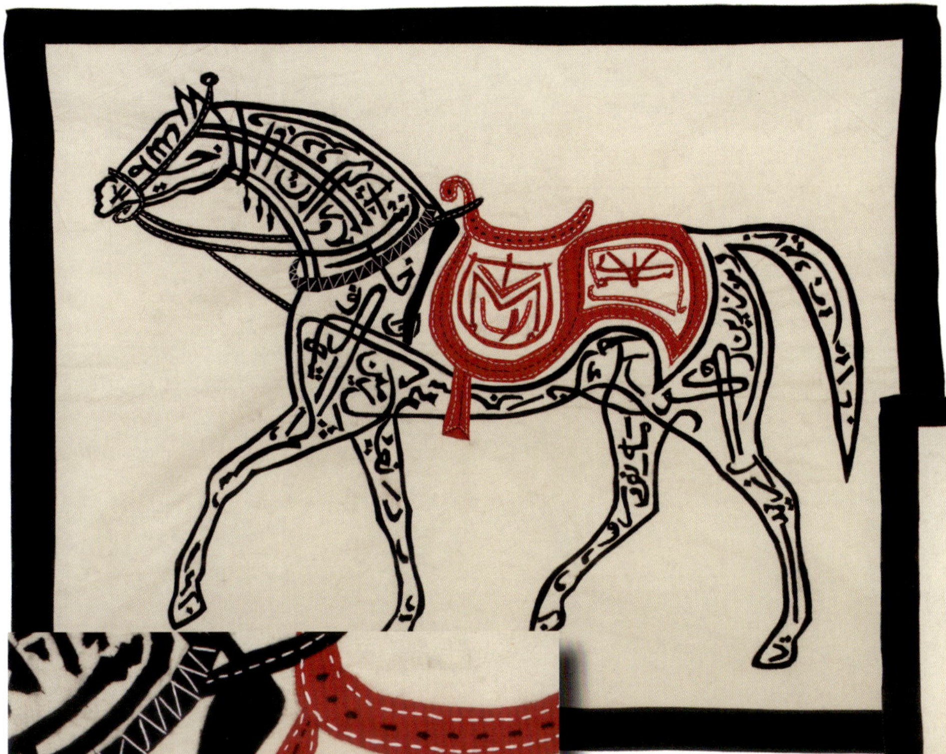

20 Ashraf Hashem

Horse in calligraphy

Black and red on white

45" x 37"

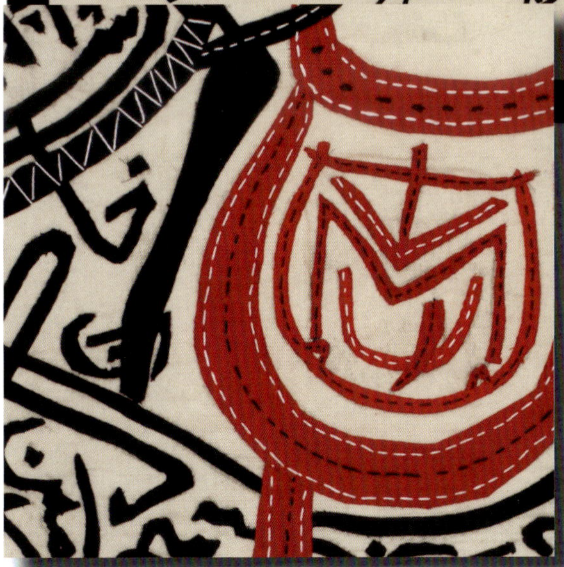

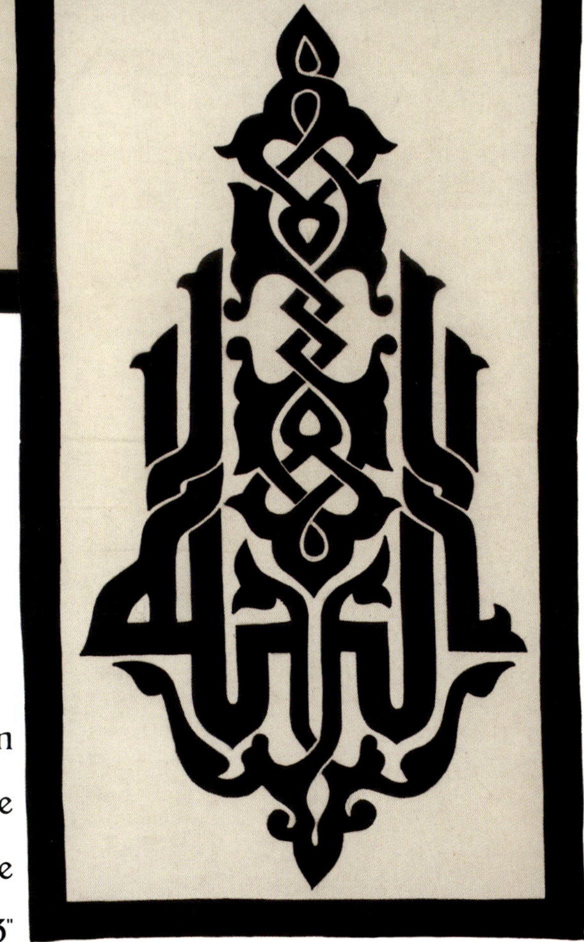

21 Ashraf Hashem

Like a Candle

Black on white

39" x 23"

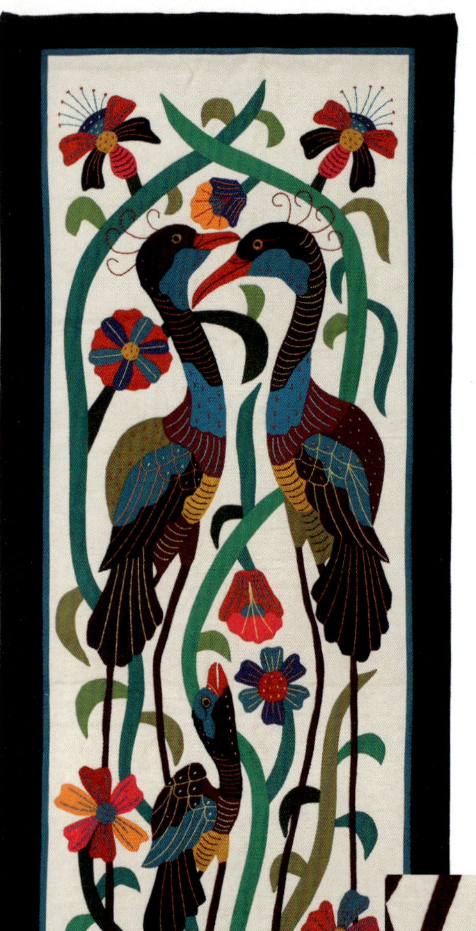

22 Ayman Molukiya

Cranes, traditional tomb image

Blue, green, and bright colors on white

20" x 39"

23 Ayman Molukiya

Small Tree of Life with birds

Greens on cream

20" x 35"

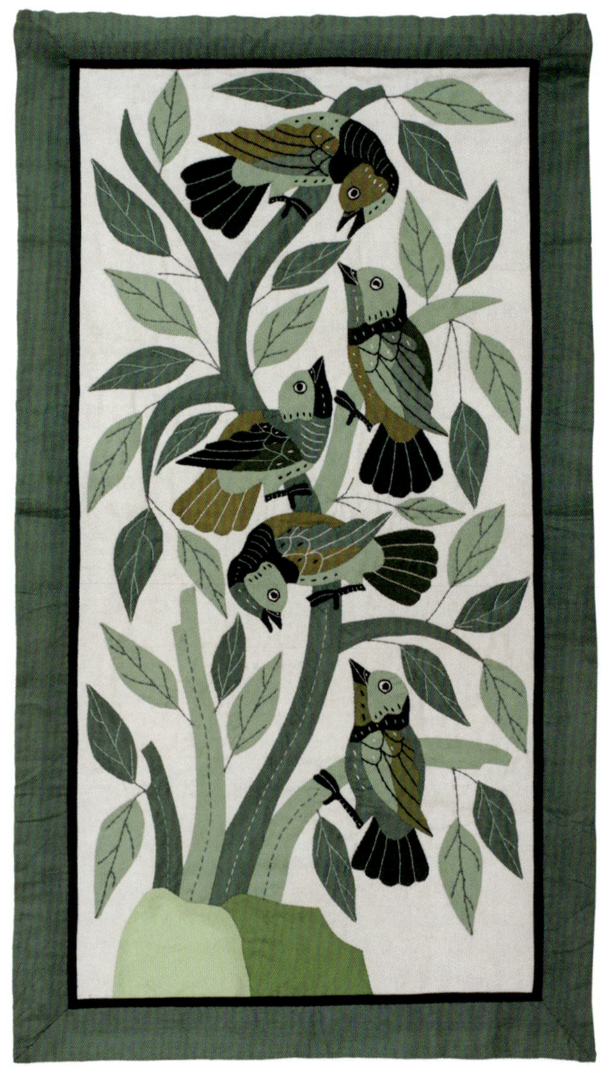

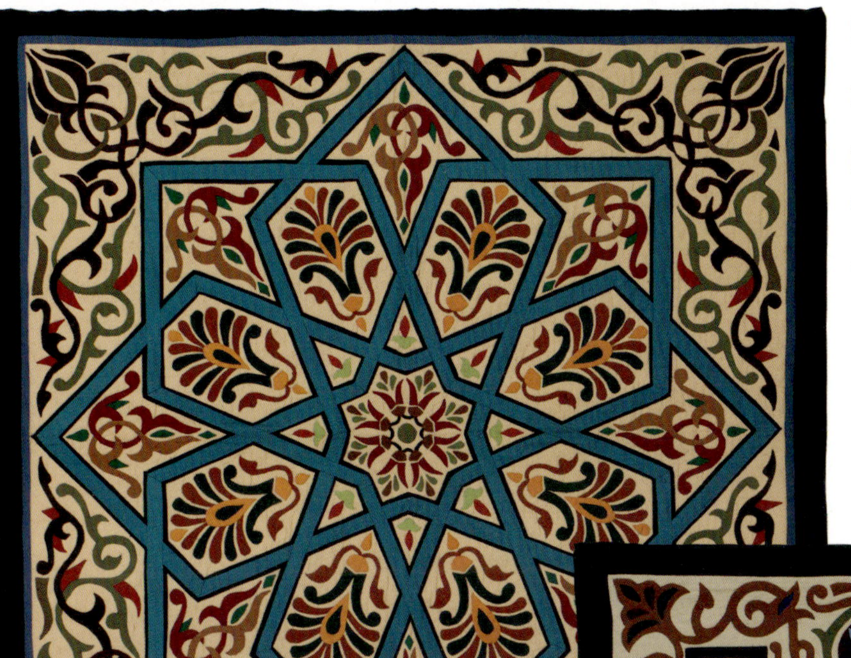

24 Gamal

Star

Blue, greens, earth
colors on light

47" x 47"

25 Gamal

Romy with Lotus design

Greens, blues and
earth colors on cream

49" x 49"

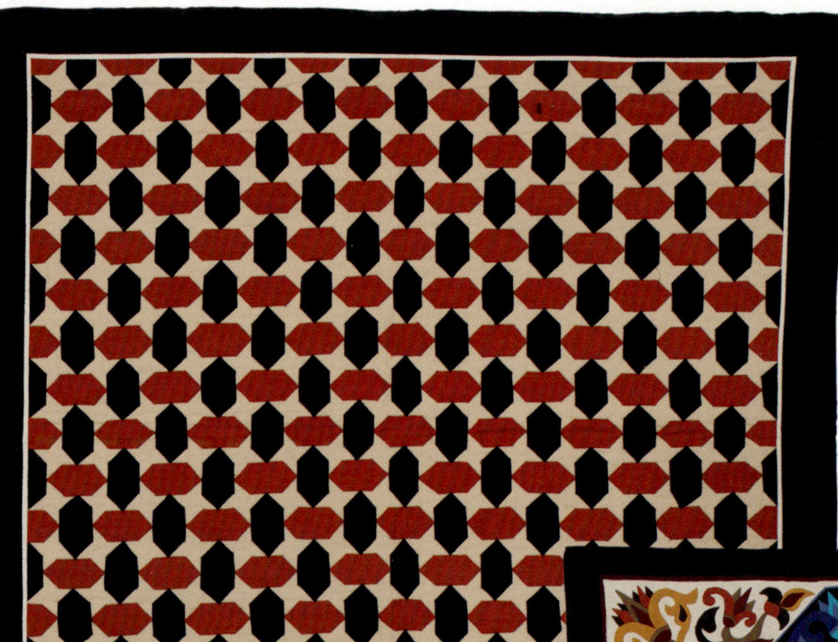

26 Gamal

Islamic design –
regular long hexagons

Zippered Floor
Pillow Cover

Navy and brick on white

31" x 31"

27 Ahmed Naguib

Star, concentrics,
and Lotus

Blues and multicol-
ors on cream

59" x 59"

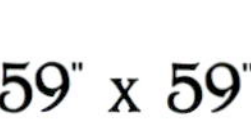

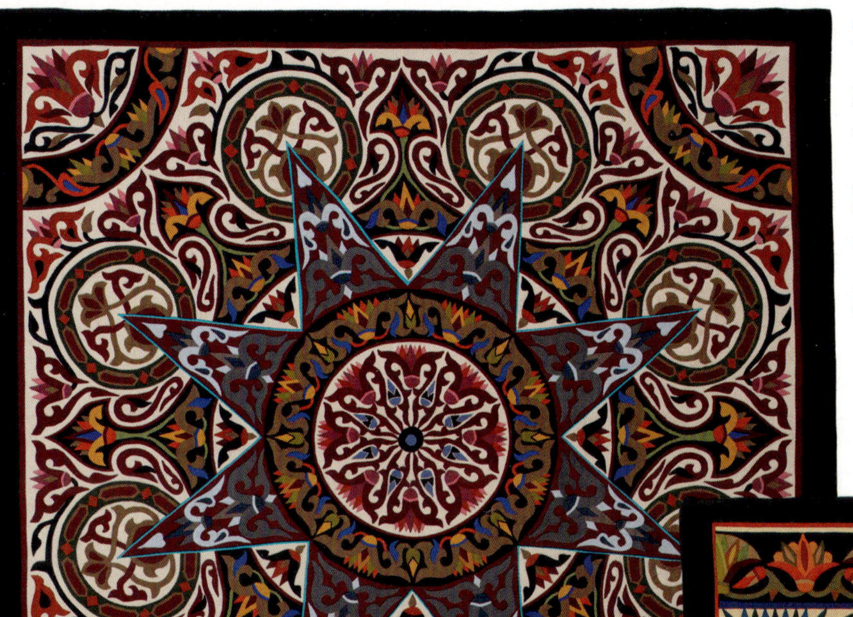

28 Ahmed Naguib

Star in Islamic patterning
with Lotus

Burgundy, green, gray,
and multicolors on cream

59" x 59"

29 Hany Abd El Khader

Complex Lotus with
parallel borders

Burgundy, green, reds,
and multicolors on
cream, navy border

43" x 51"

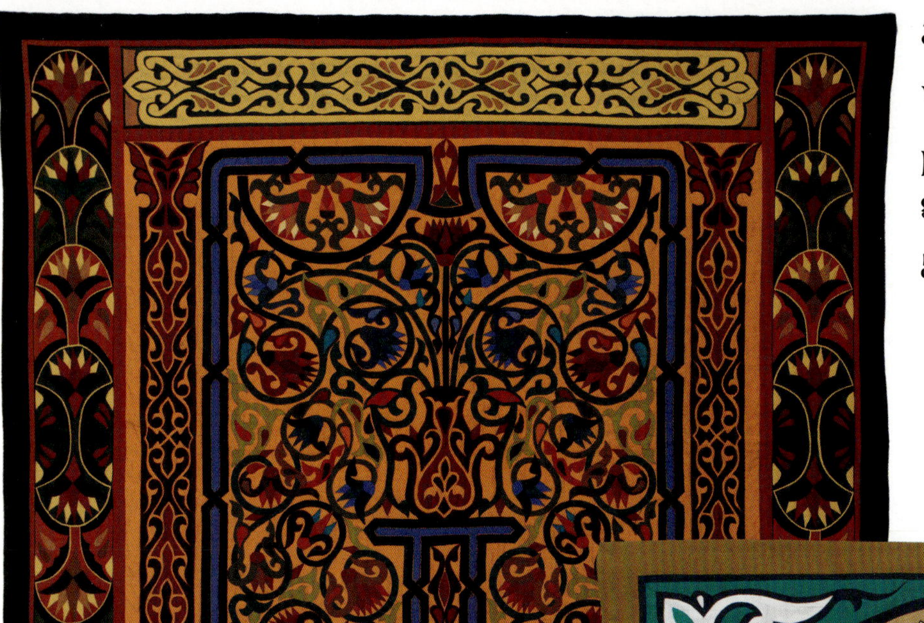

30 Hany Abd El Khader

Vase on stand with Lotus

Blues and reds and greens on gold

55" x 59"

31 Essam Ali

Geometric Islamic design

Turquoise and green with black linework

39" x 39"

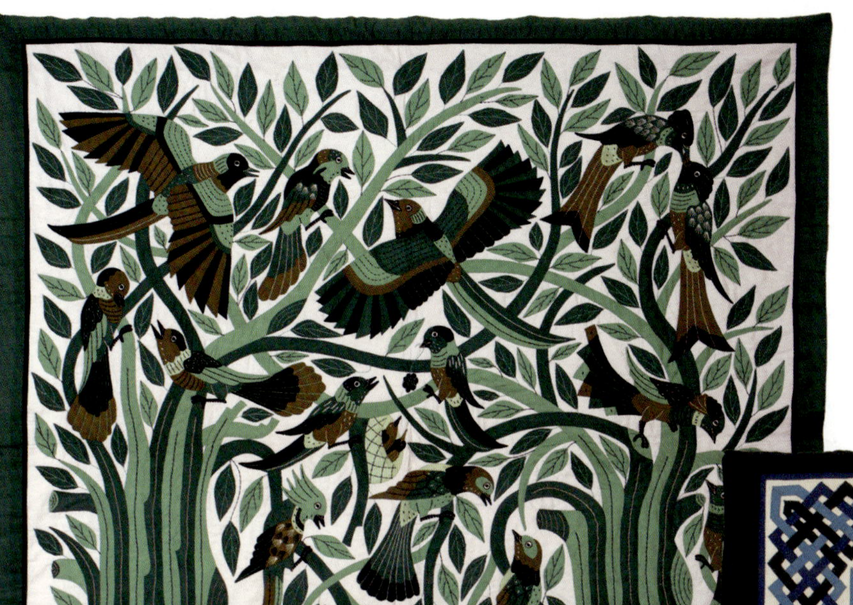

32 Tarek Fattoh

Tree of Life

Green tree with birds

59" x 59"

33 Tarek Fattoh

Romy Design with
Lattice border

Blues on white

43" x 35"

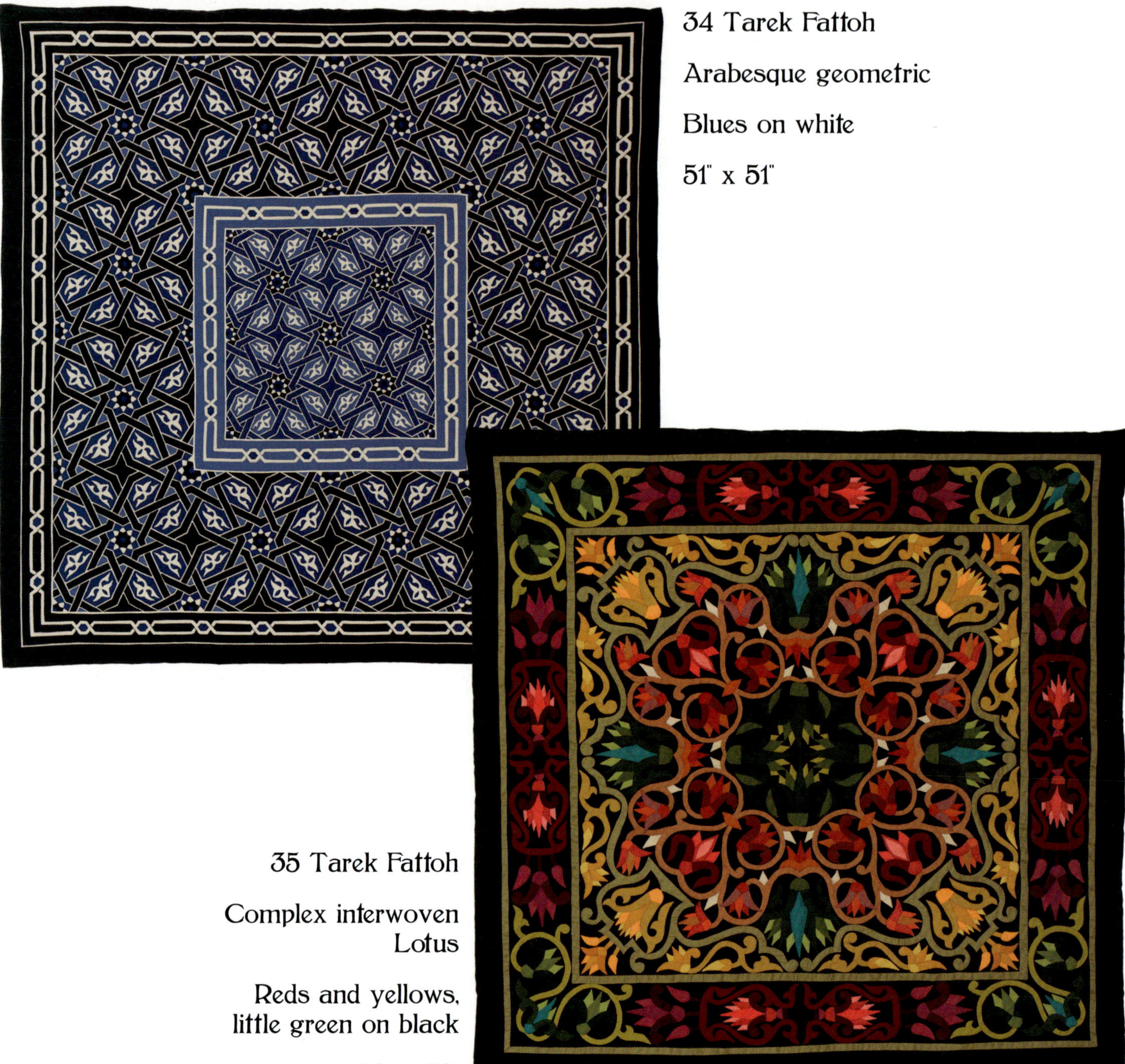

34 Tarek Fattoh

Arabesque geometric

Blues on white

51" x 51"

35 Tarek Fattoh

Complex interwoven
Lotus

Reds and yellows,
little green on black

39" x 39"

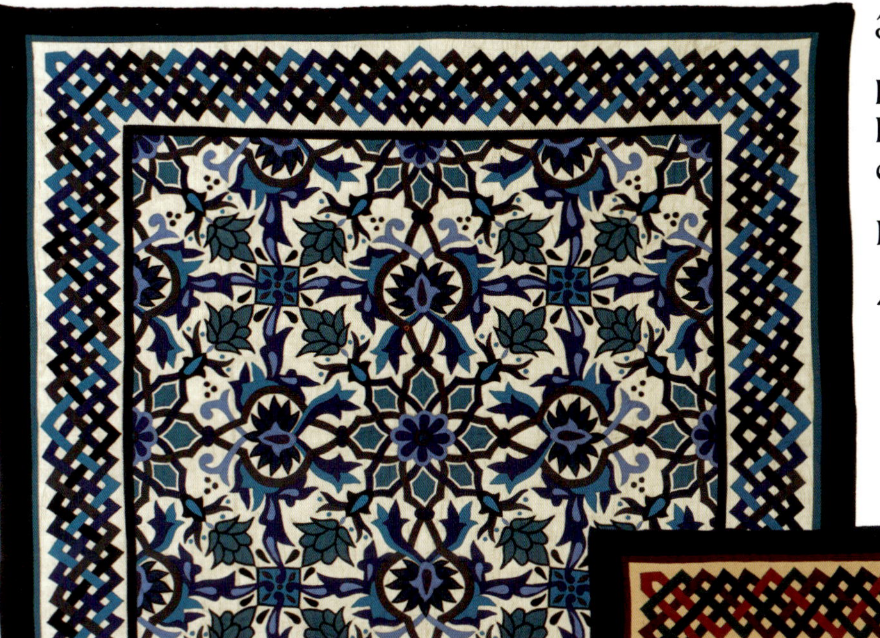

36 Tarek Fattoh

Double flower with
lattice border and
embroidered details

Blues and white

43" x 43"

37 Tarek Fattoh

Double flower with
lattice border and
embroidered details

Terracotta and navy
on dark beige

43" x 43"

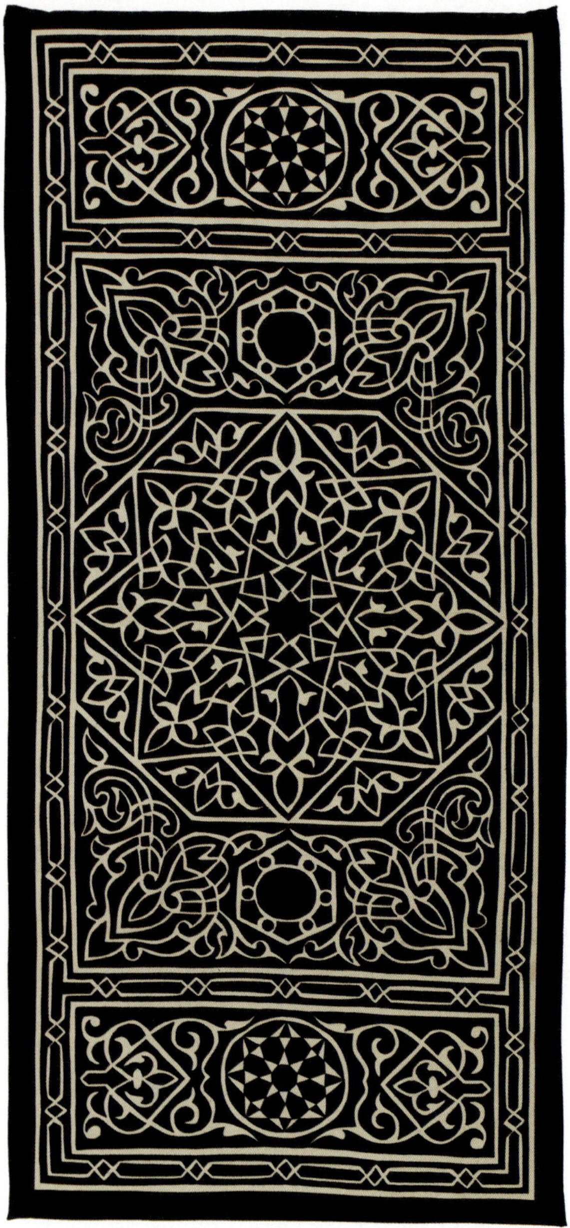

38 Tarek Fattoh

Islamic mosque
door design

Navy on cream

33" x 74"

39 Tarek Fattoh

Simple Lotus

Tawny browns and
greens on cream

39" x 51"

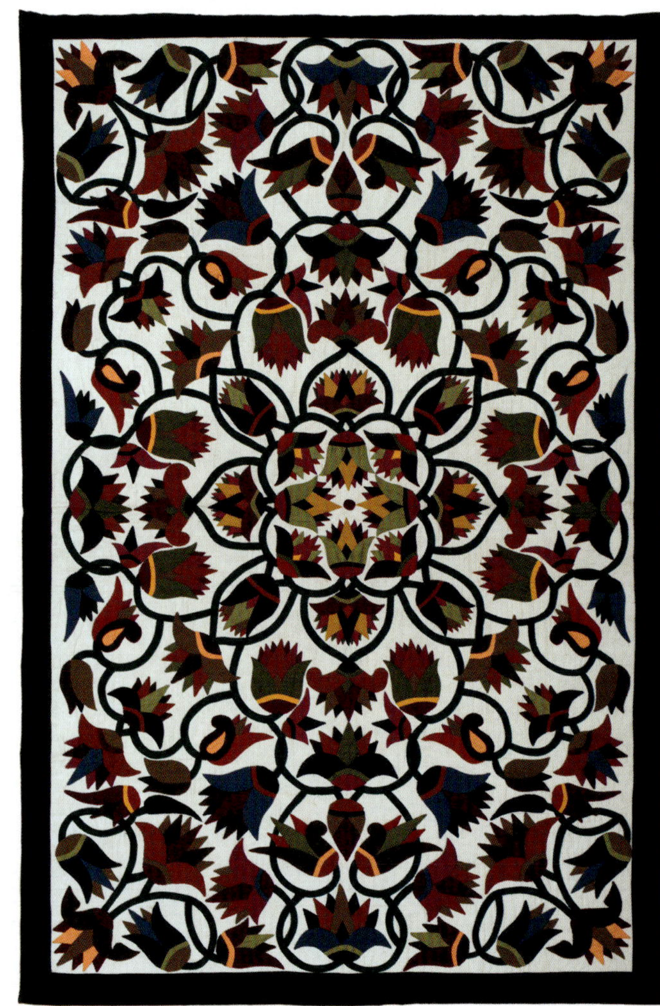

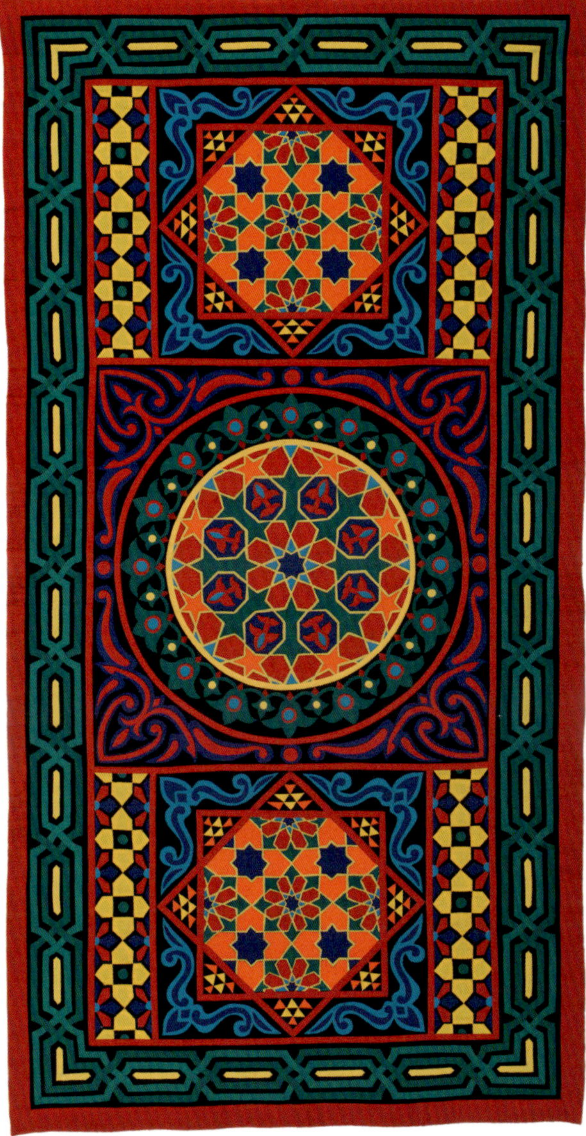

40 Tarek Fattoh

Traditional Islamic – street screen style

Very bright primaries

39" x 78"

41 Tarek Fattoh

Traditional Lotus

Navy blue and terracotta

39" x 78"

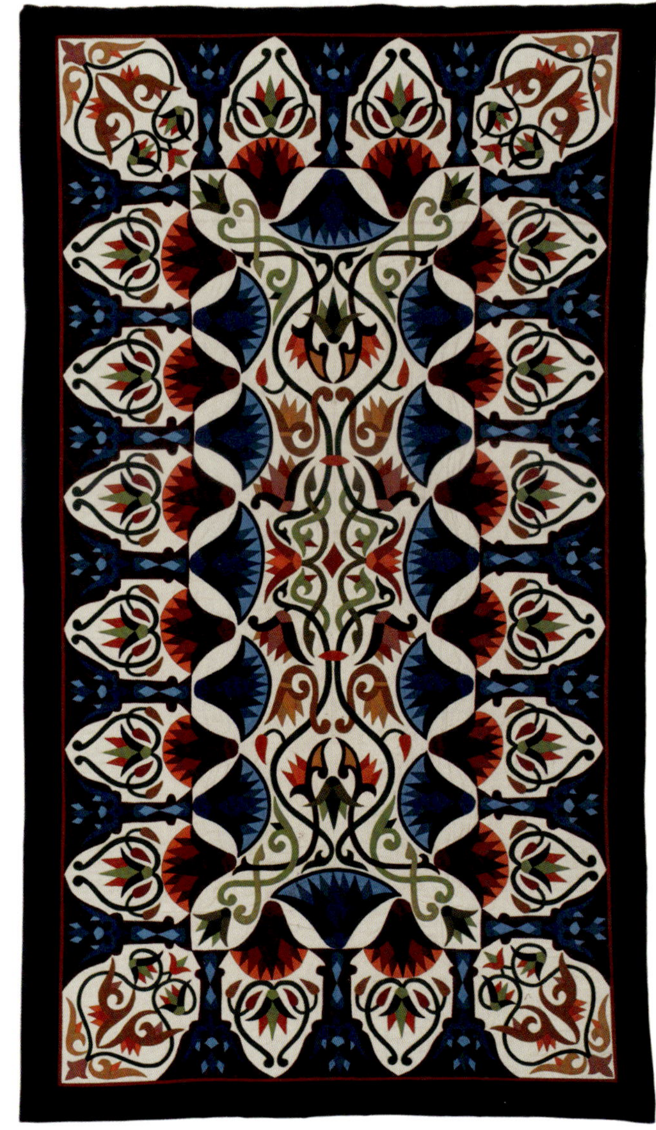

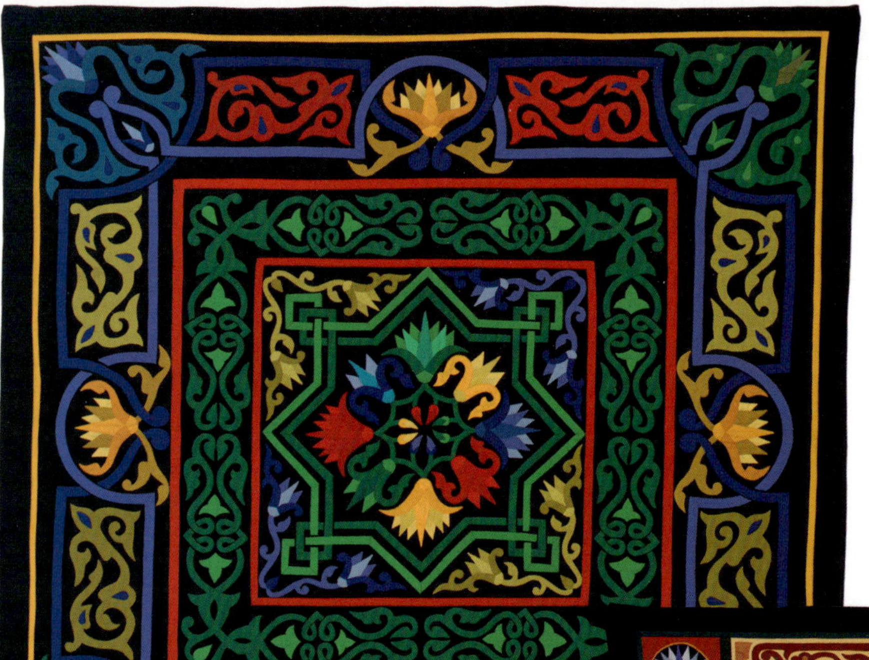

42 Tarek Fattoh

Lotus, Romy and Islamic geometric linework

Jade, scarlet and blues on black

51" x 51"

43 Tarek Fattoh

Lotus, Romy vase on stand

Red, gold, and green on black

62" x 55"

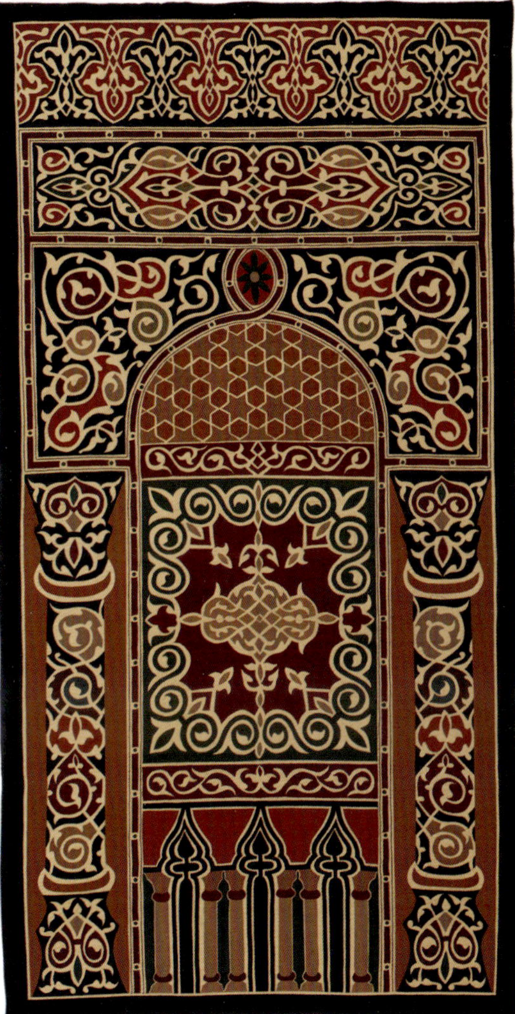

44 Tarek Fattoh

Mihrab – the curved niche in a mosque in inlaid stonework

Navy, red, gold, and green on dark cream

39" x 75"

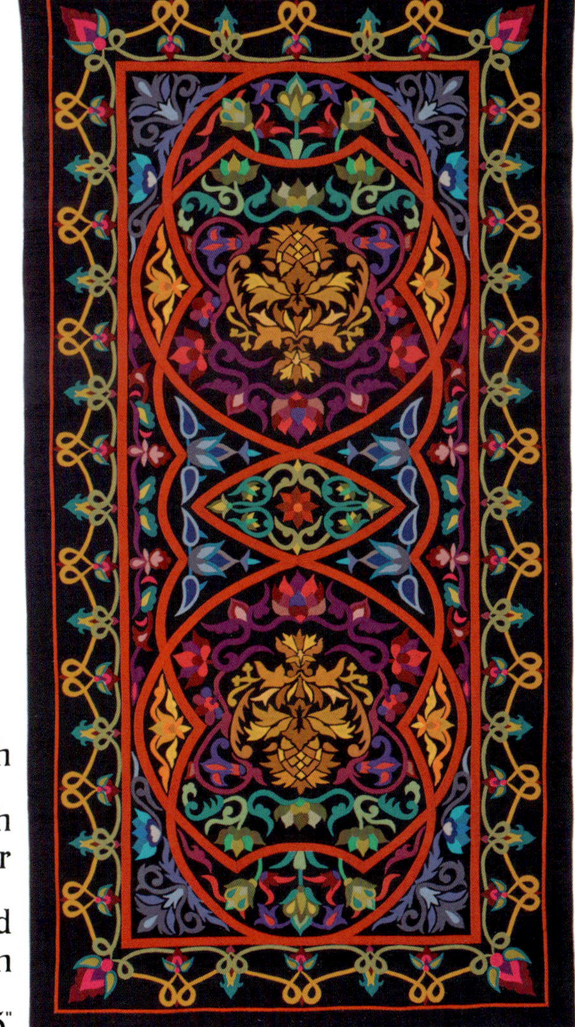

45 Tarek Fattoh

Flowers and pines with looped border

Navy, red, gold, and green on dark cream

39" x 75"

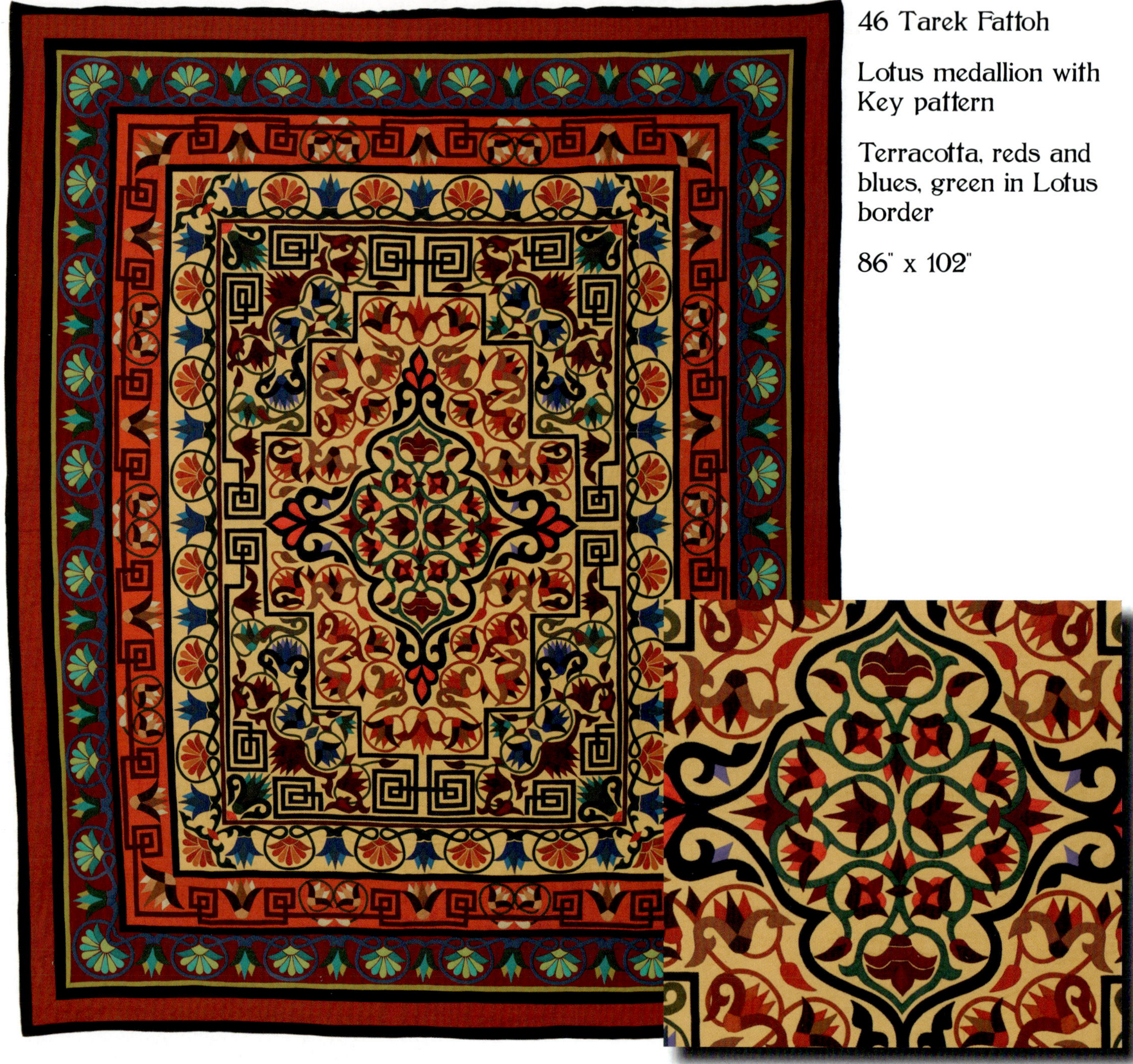

46 Tarek Fattoh

Lotus medallion with Key pattern

Terracotta, reds and blues, green in Lotus border

86" x 102"

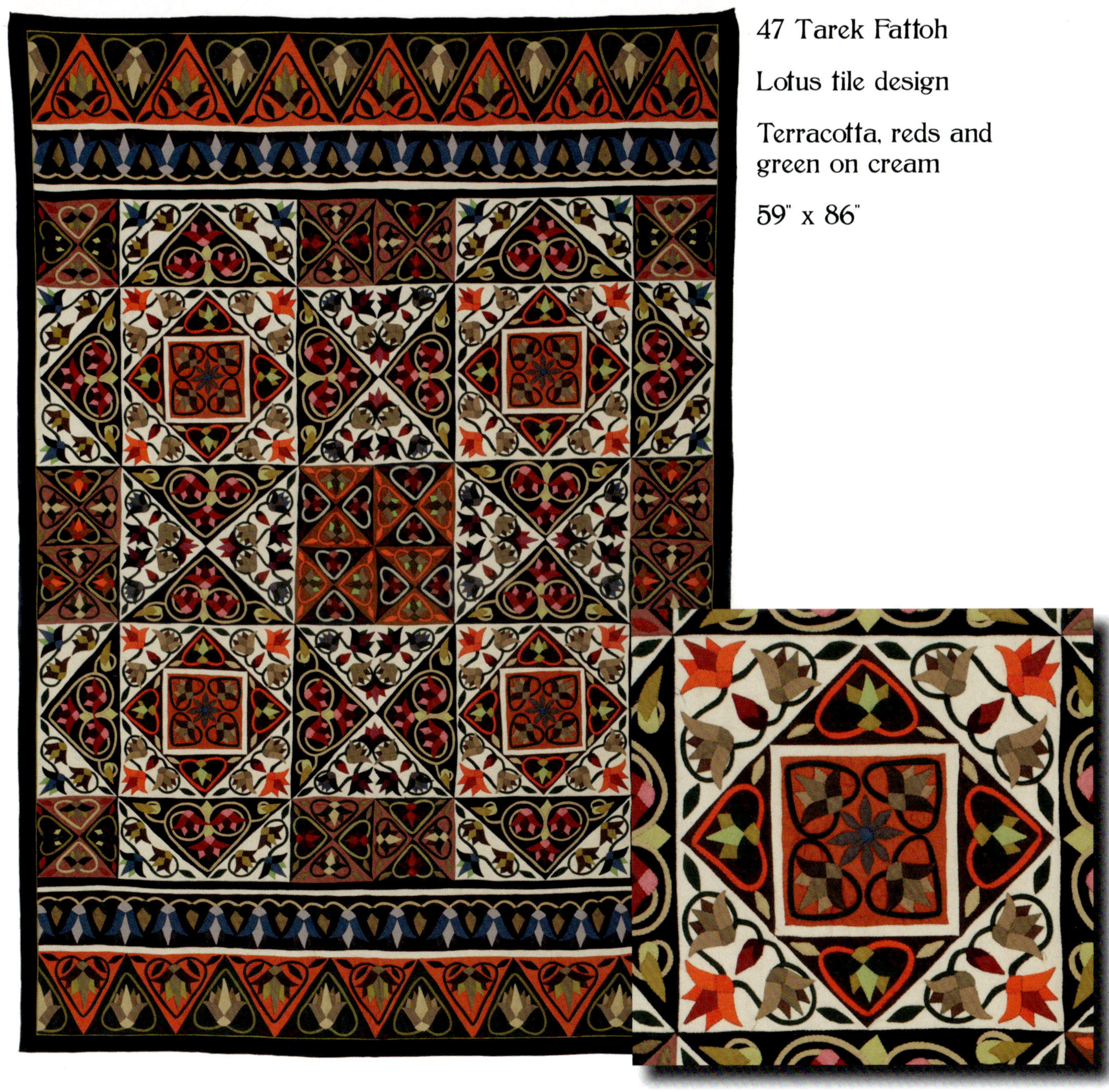

47 Tarek Fattoh

Lotus tile design

Terracotta, reds and green on cream

59" x 86"

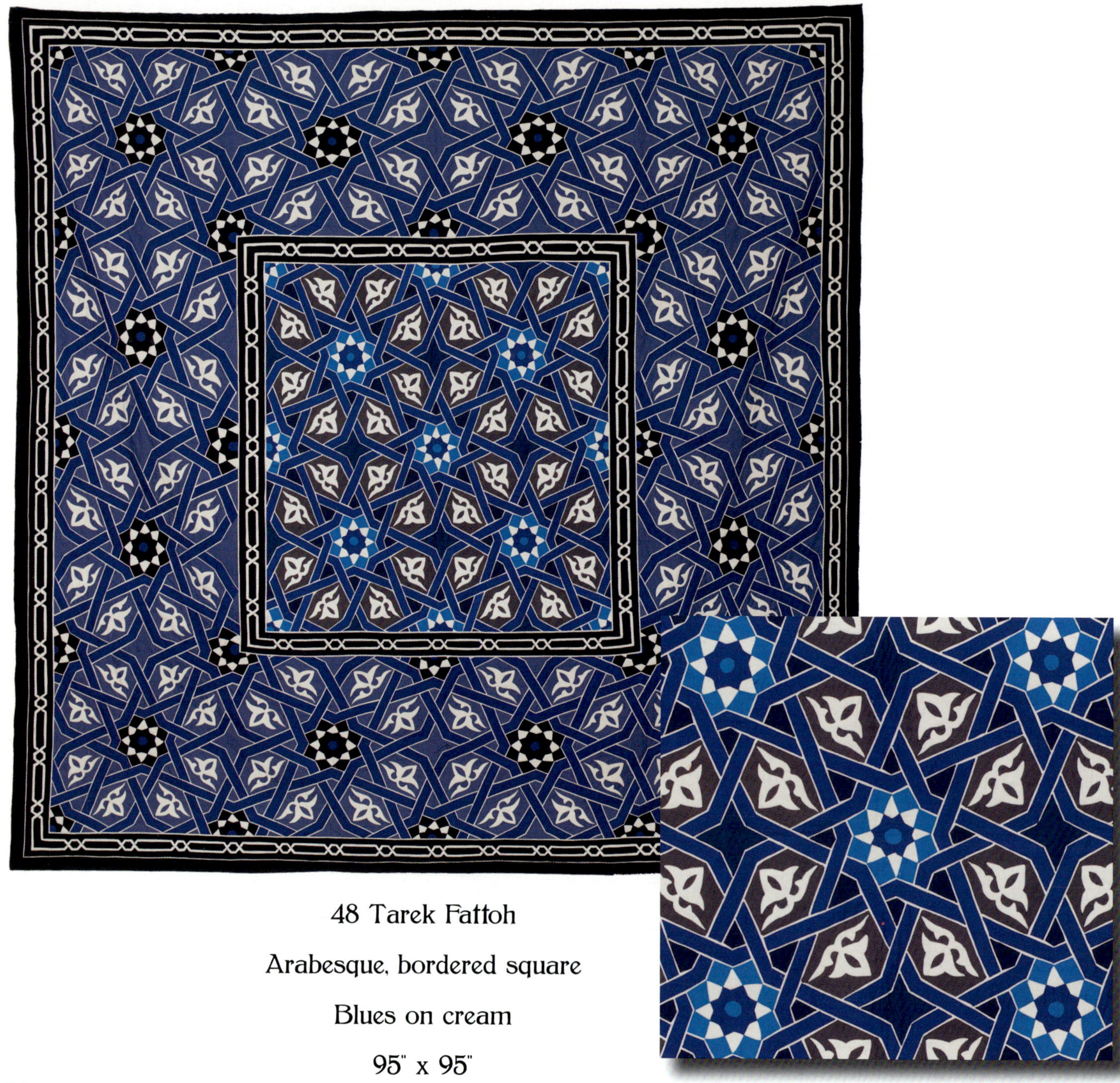

48 Tarek Fattoh

Arabesque, bordered square

Blues on cream

95" x 95"

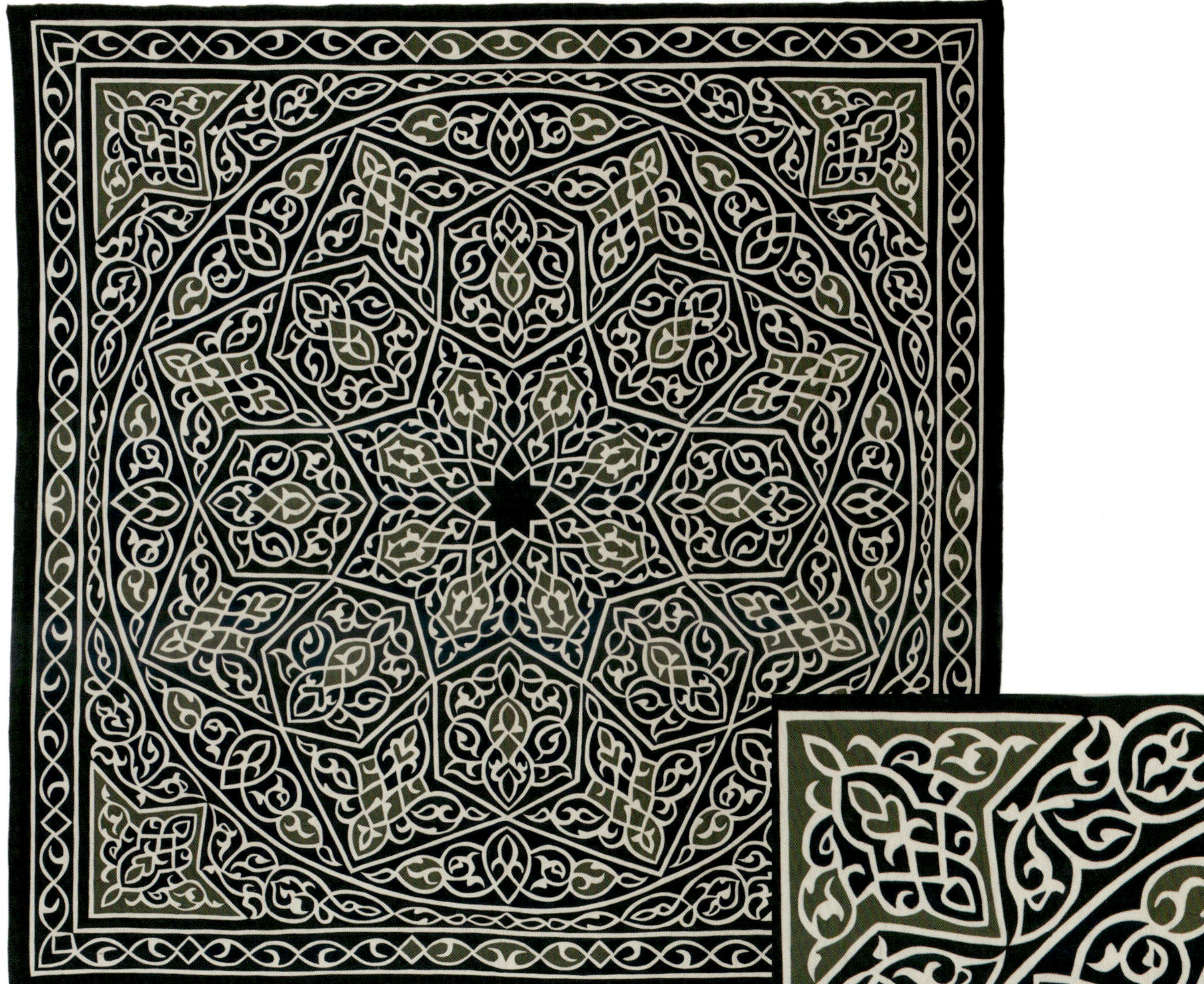

49 Tarek Fattoh

Traditional Islamic

Green on cream

100" x 100"

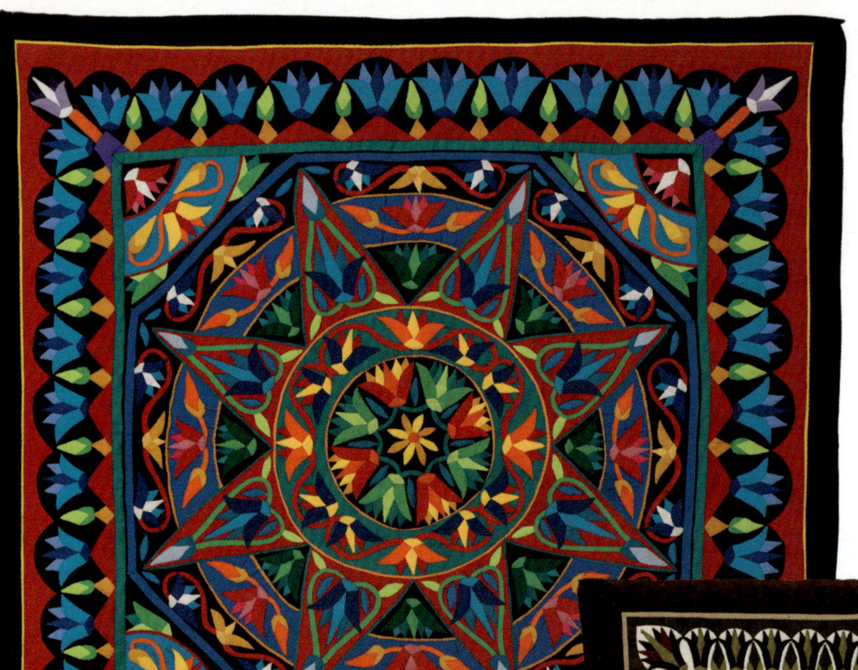

50 Tarek Fattoh

Lotus Star with Lotus border

Bright primaries and multicolors on black

39" x 39"

51 Tarek Fattoh

Lotus Star with fine Lotus border

Olive and tan on cream

39" x 39"

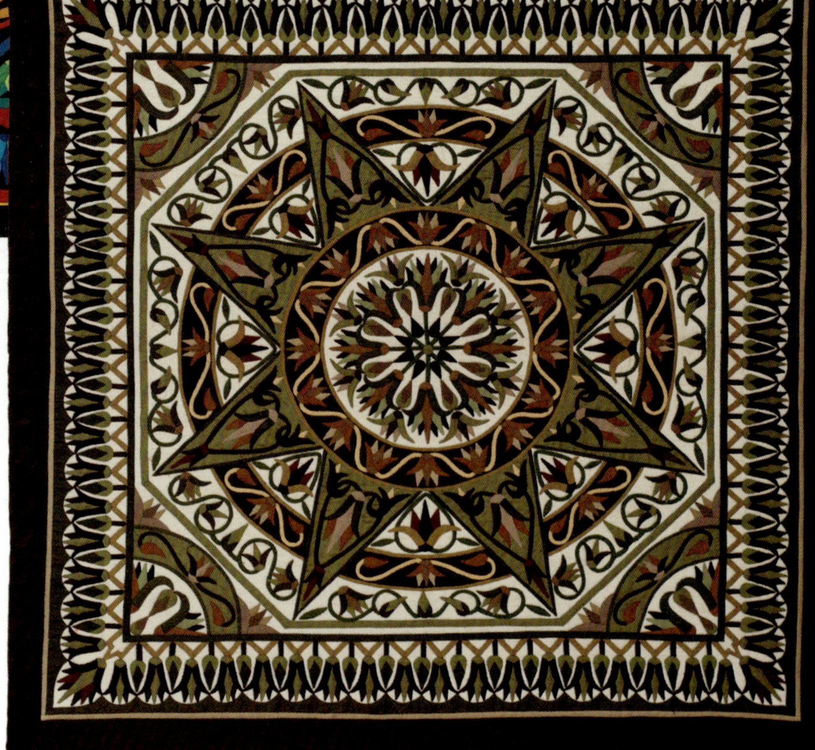

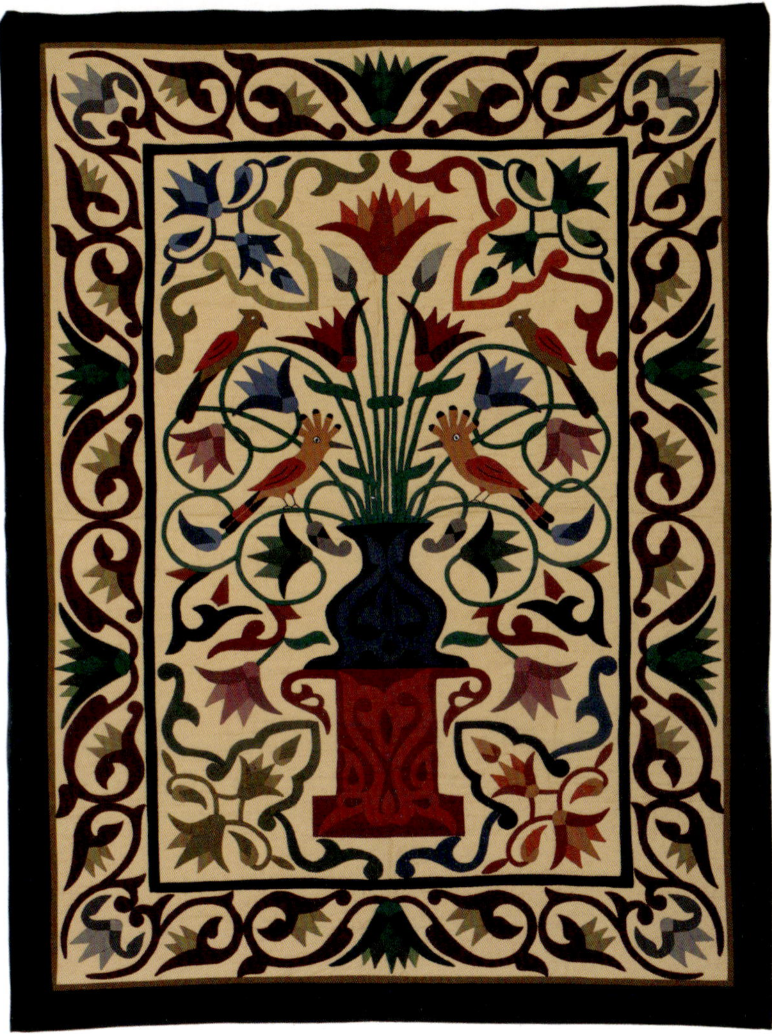

52 Tarek Fattoh

Hoopoes with flowers
in vase

Multicolors on cream

31" x 43"

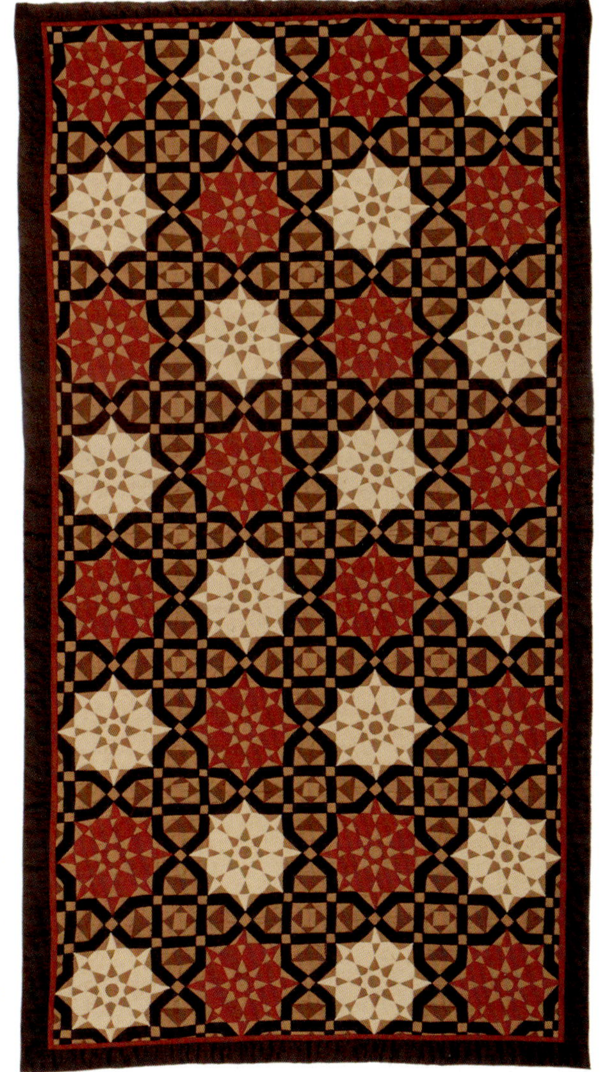

53 Tarek Fattoh

Arabesque

Browns on cream

35" x 63"

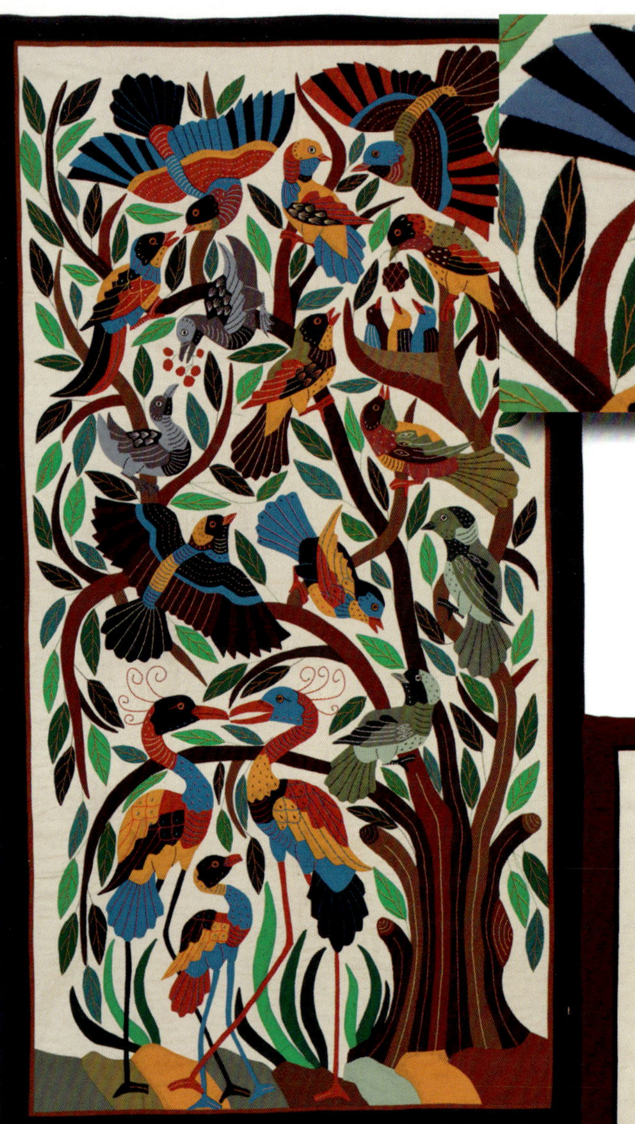

54 Tarek Fattoh

Tree of Life

Brights on cream

35" x 67"

55 Hosam Al Farouk, stitched by Mohamed Ota

Horse Calligraphy

Black on white with pink, blue, and aqua

47" x 39"

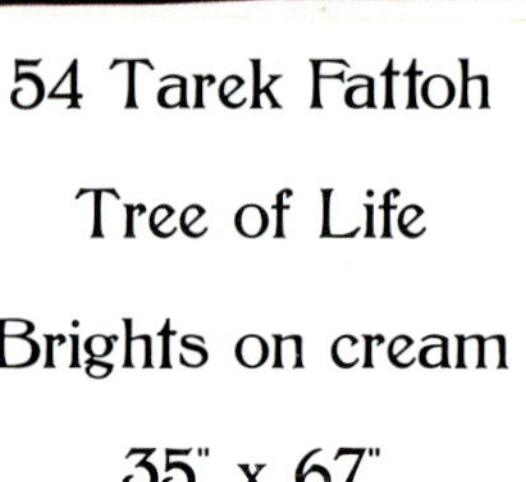

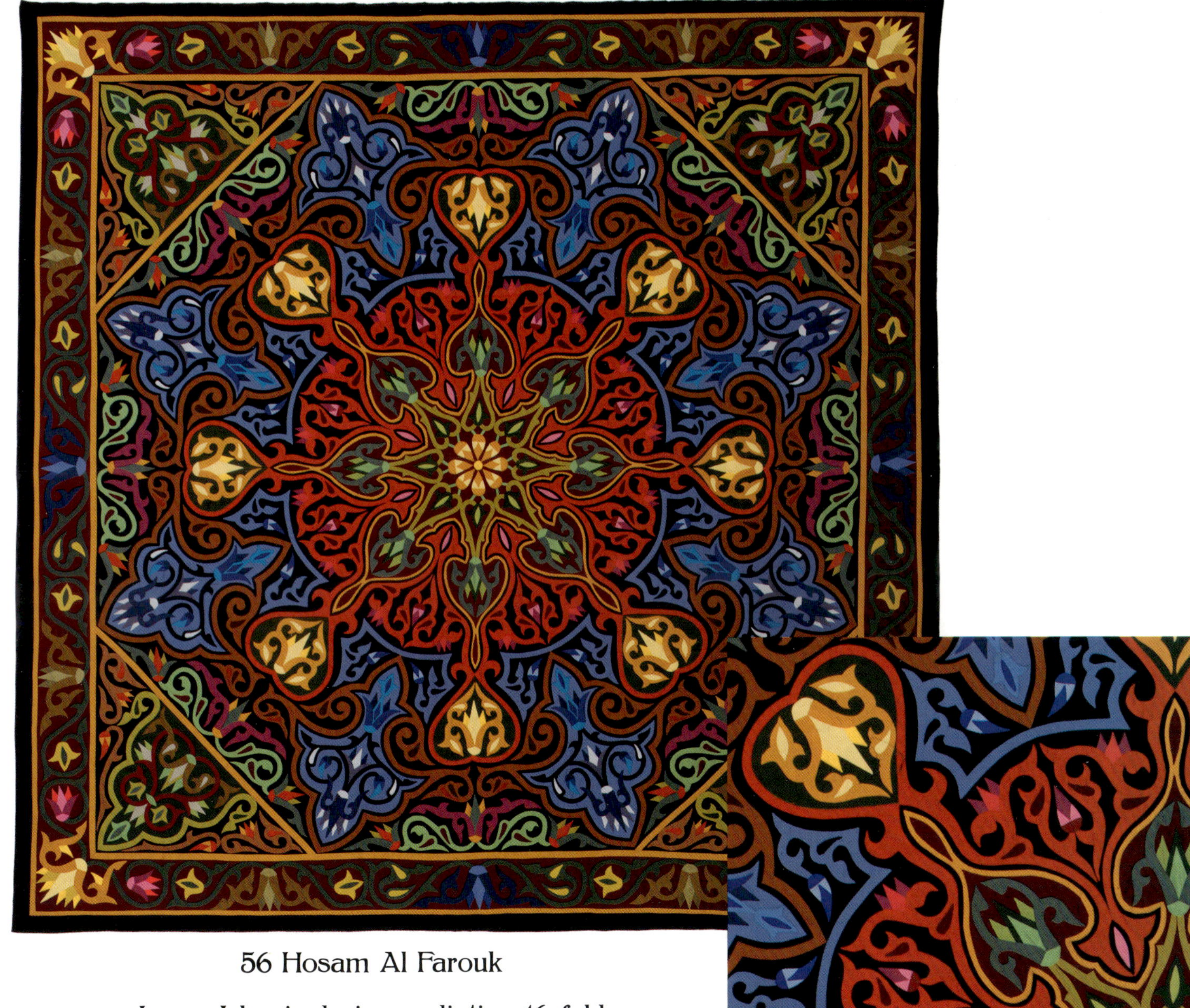

56 Hosam Al Farouk

Large Islamic design, radiating 16–fold

Red, yellow, blue, green on black

98" x 98"

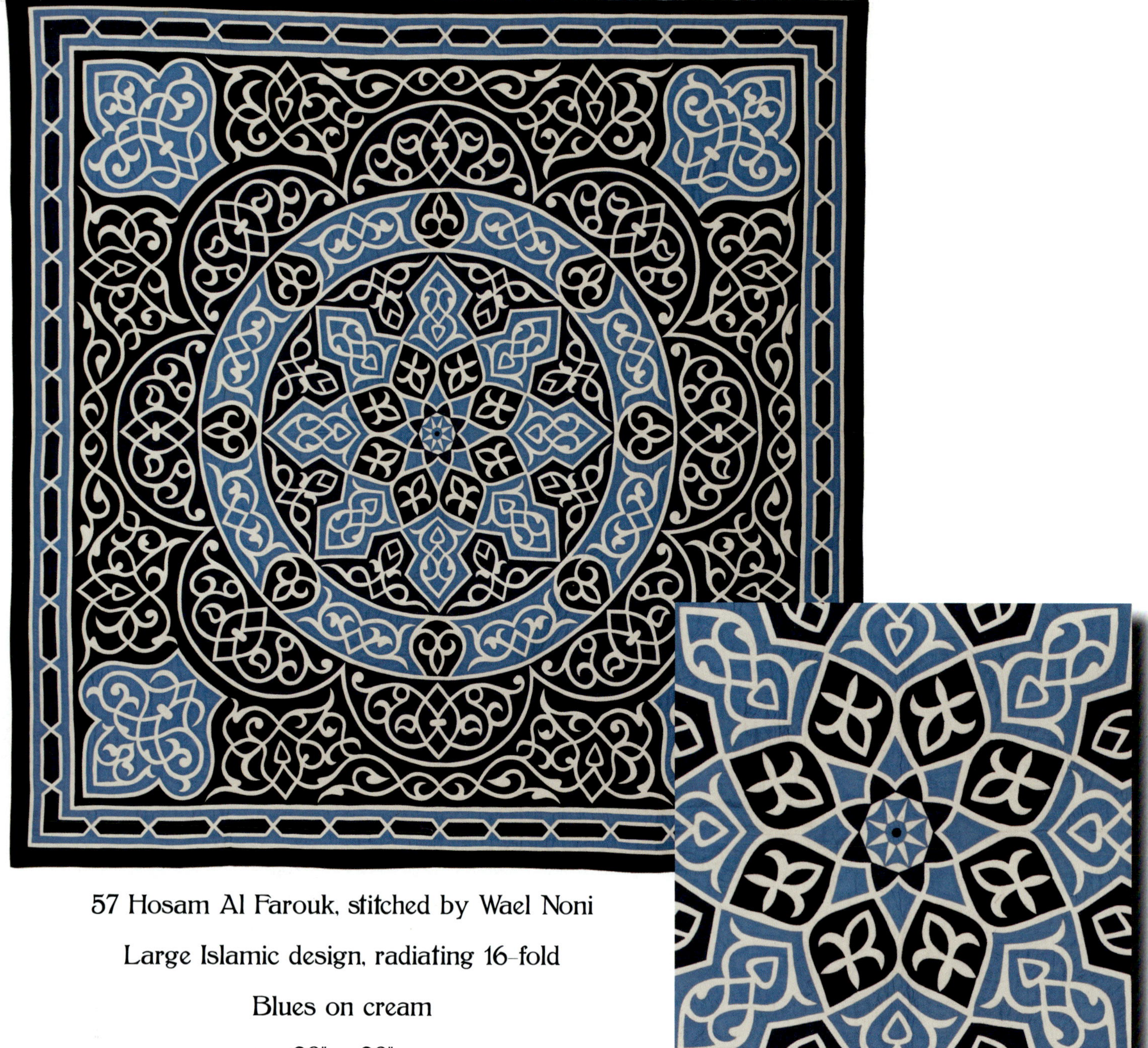

57 Hosam Al Farouk, stitched by Wael Noni

Large Islamic design, radiating 16–fold

Blues on cream

98" x 98"

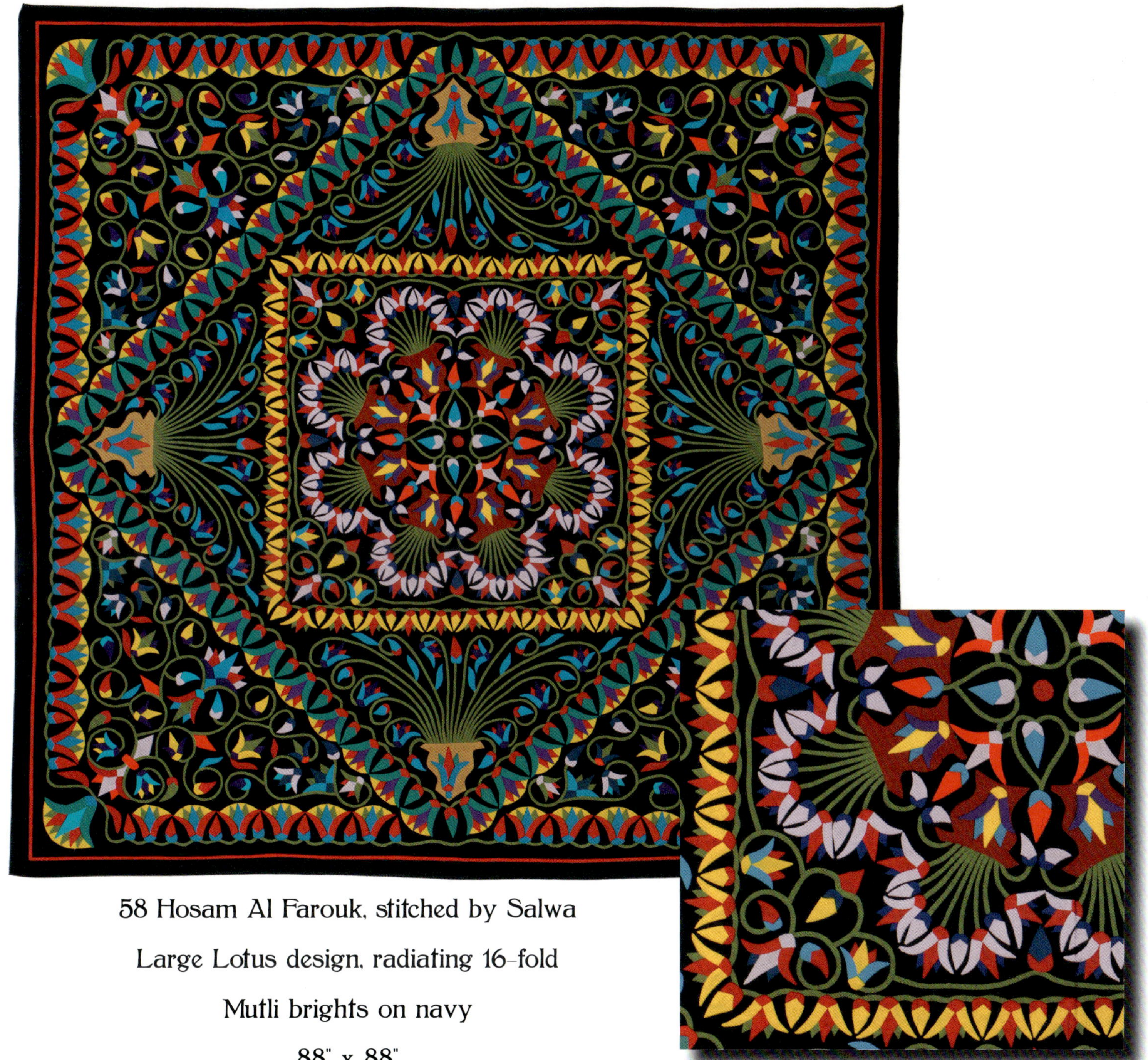

58 Hosam Al Farouk, stitched by Salwa

Large Lotus design, radiating 16-fold

Mutli brights on navy

88" x 88"

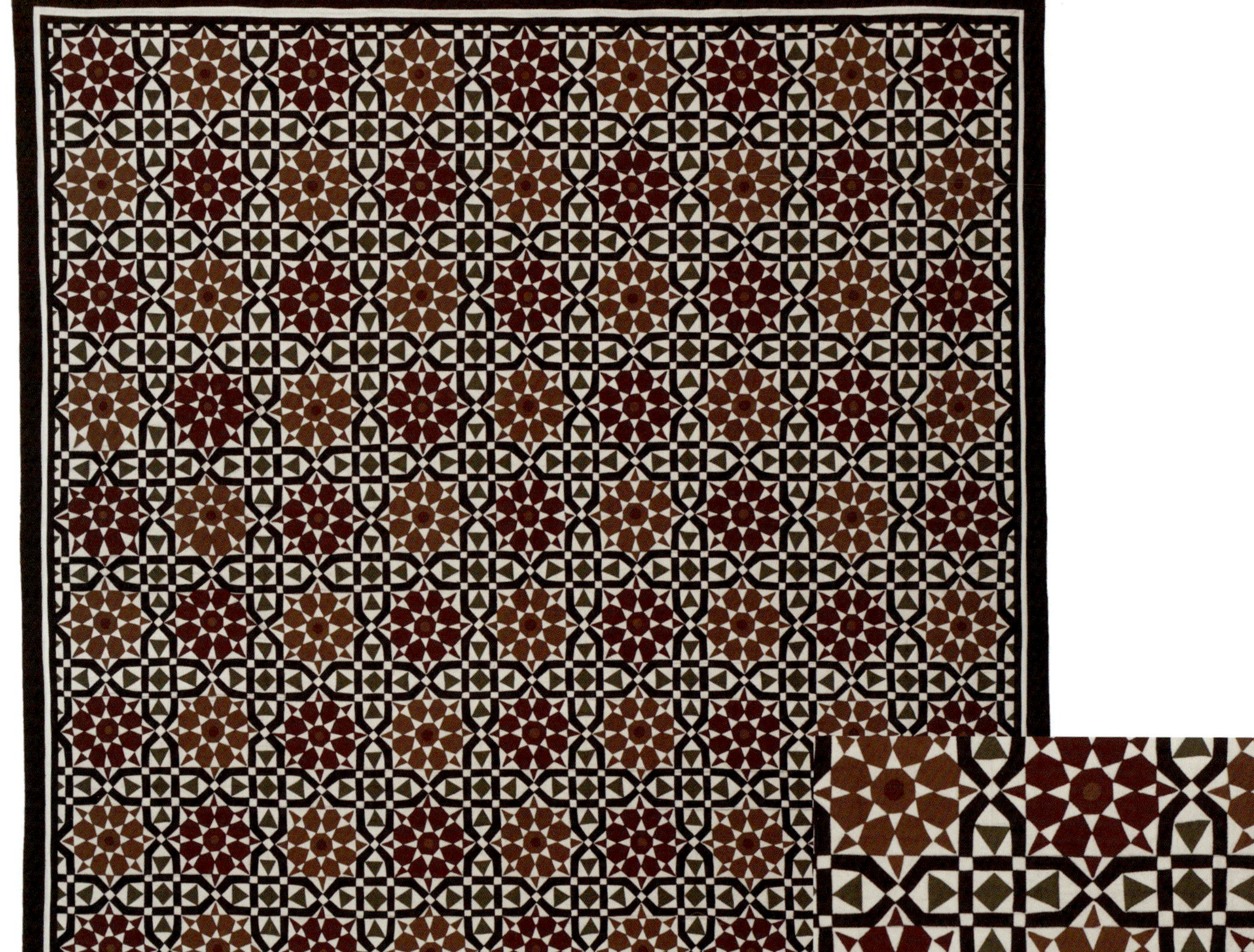

59 Hosam Al Farouk, stitched by Mutaz

Arabesque

Brown and olive on white

88" x 88"

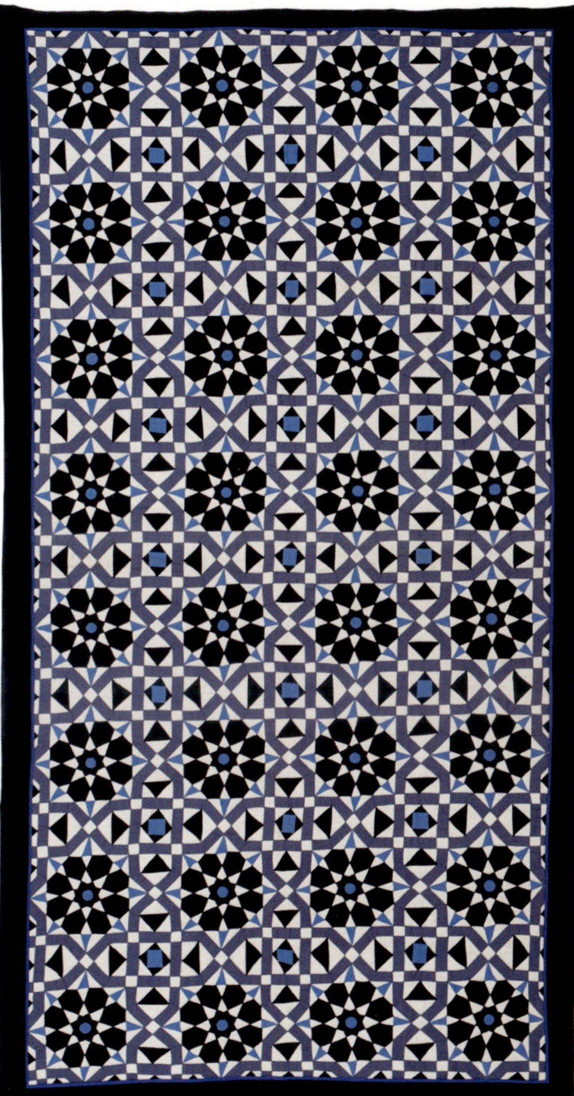

60 Hosam Al Farouk,
stitched by Farouk

Arabesque

Blues on white

39" x 70"

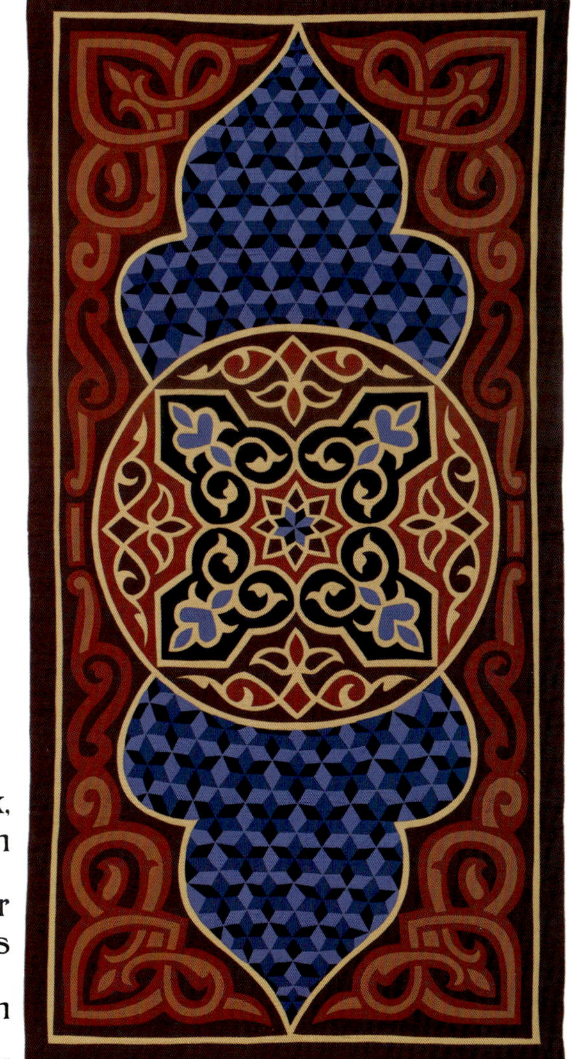

61 Hosam Al Farouk,
stitched by Hassan

Islamic door design, center
medallion and stars

Blues and brown

39" x 78"

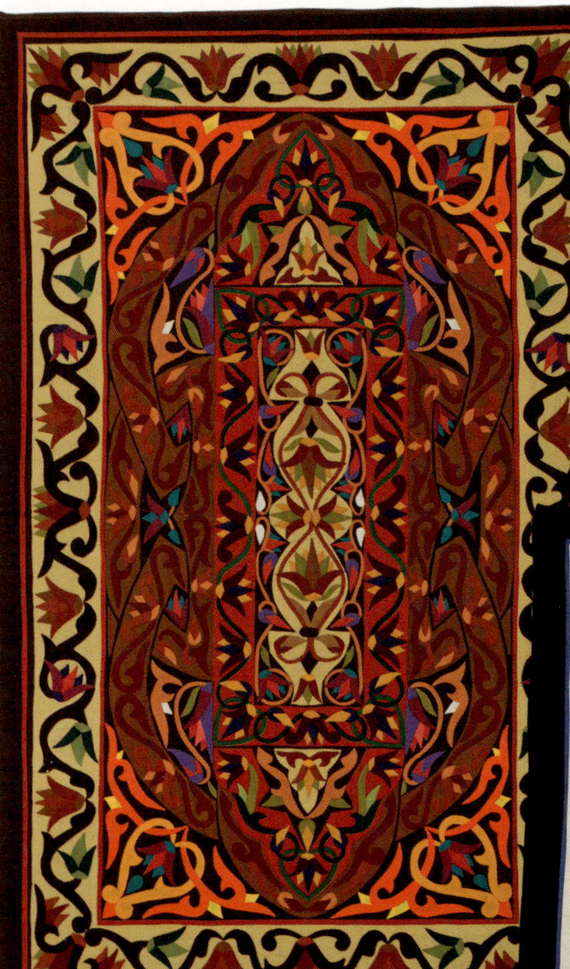

62 Hosam Al Farouk
stitched by Wafa'a

Lotus and Romy
design

Purple and orange
with brown

39" x 63"

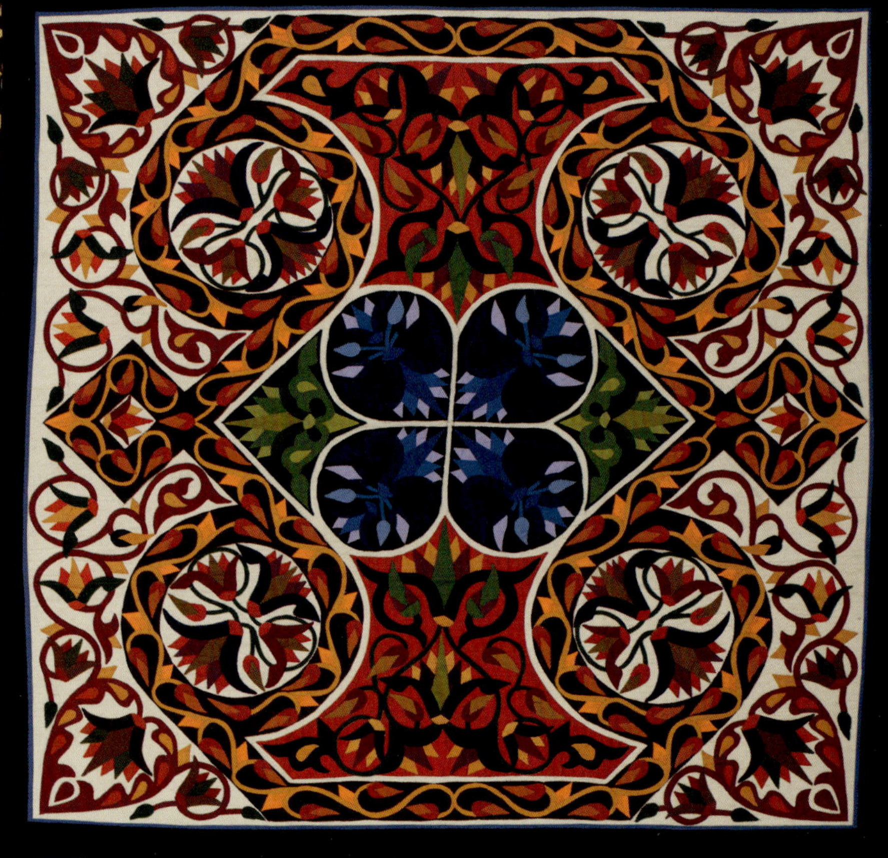

63 Hosam Al Farouk,
stitched by Mahmoud

Unusual Lotus and Islamic design

Blue, gold, and multicolors on two
backgrounds, outer white

47" x 47"

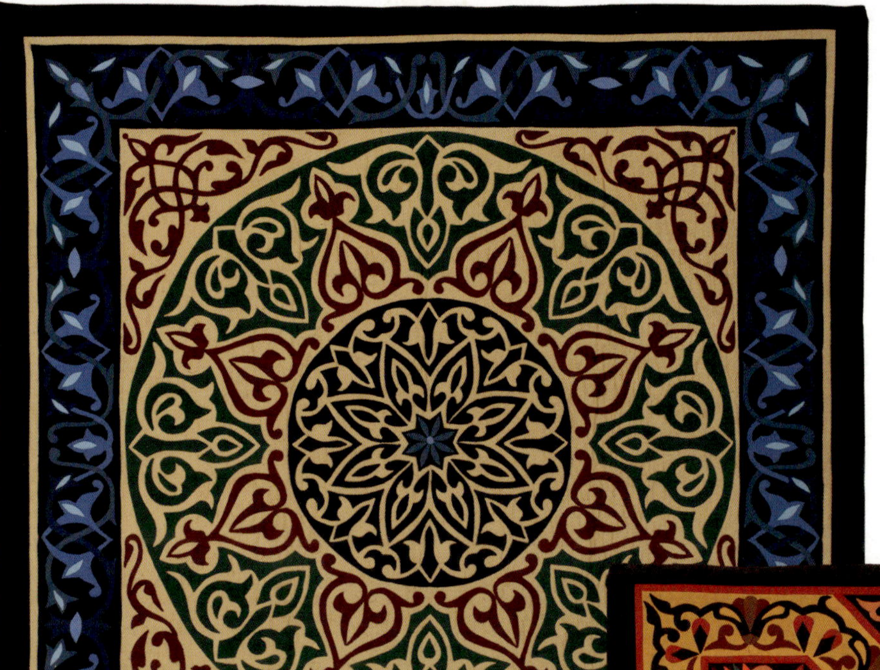

64 Hosam Al Farouk,
stitched by Mido

Traditional Romy
on Beige

Blue, red, and green
on beige

47" x 47"

65 Hosam Al Farouk,
stitched by Mido

Lotus, Romy and Islamic
design with medallion

Gold, red, brown, and
green on dark

47" x 47"

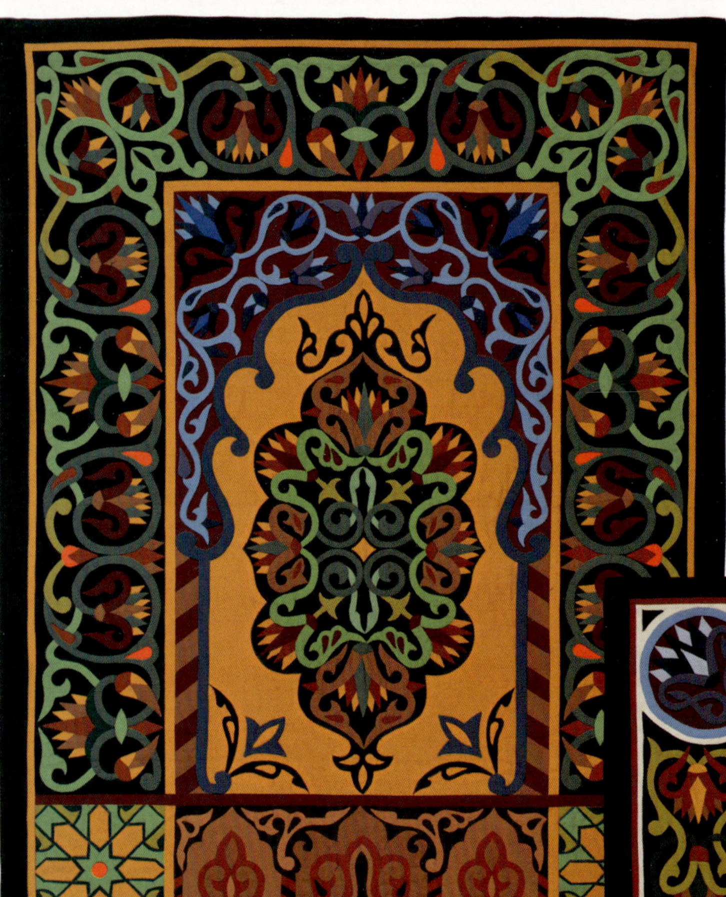

66 Hosam Al Farouk, stitched by Sayed

Mihrab – niche-style design

Multicolor on yellow and dark background

39" x 49"

67 Hosam Al Farouk, stitched by Abdeen

Lotus and Romy Design

Green and multicolor on light and dark backgrounds

47" x 47"

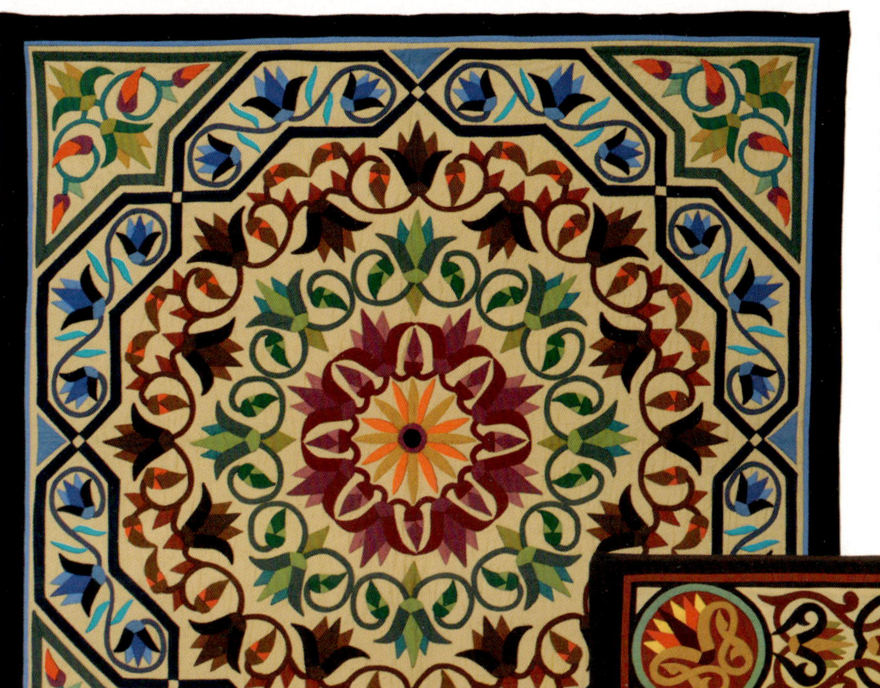

68 Hosam Al Farouk, stitched by Amira

Lotus in concentric ring, 16–fold design– Blue, green, brown on cream background

39" x 39"

69 Hosam Al Farouk, stitched by Wael

Lotus with border, eight–fold design

Browns, greens and aqua on double background

47" x 47"

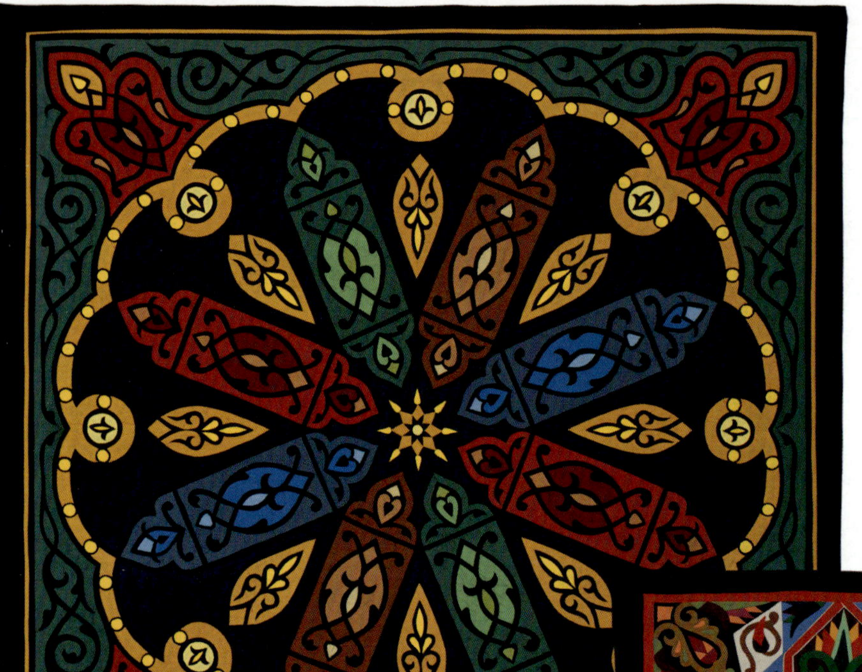

70 Hosam Al Farouk,
stitched by Wael

Islamic glass window
design

Red, blue, yellow, green,
brown on purple

55" x 55"

71 Hosam Al Farouk,
stitched by Mahmoud

Geometric with Lotus,
Eight-Point Star

Multicolors

51" x 51"

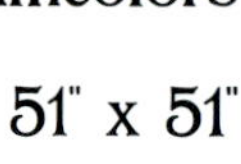

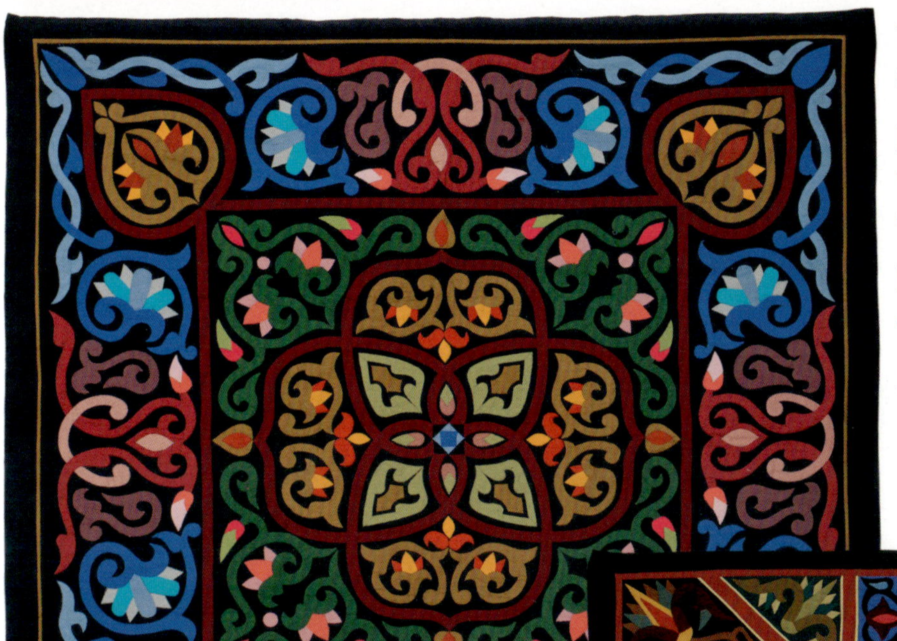

72 Hosam Al Farouk,
stitched by Mohamed

Flowers and Lotus
with border, eight–fold
design

Blue, pink, green, gold
on navy background

39" x 39"

73 Hosam Al Farouk

Geometric with Lotus

Browns, greens, and blue
on double background

47" x 47"

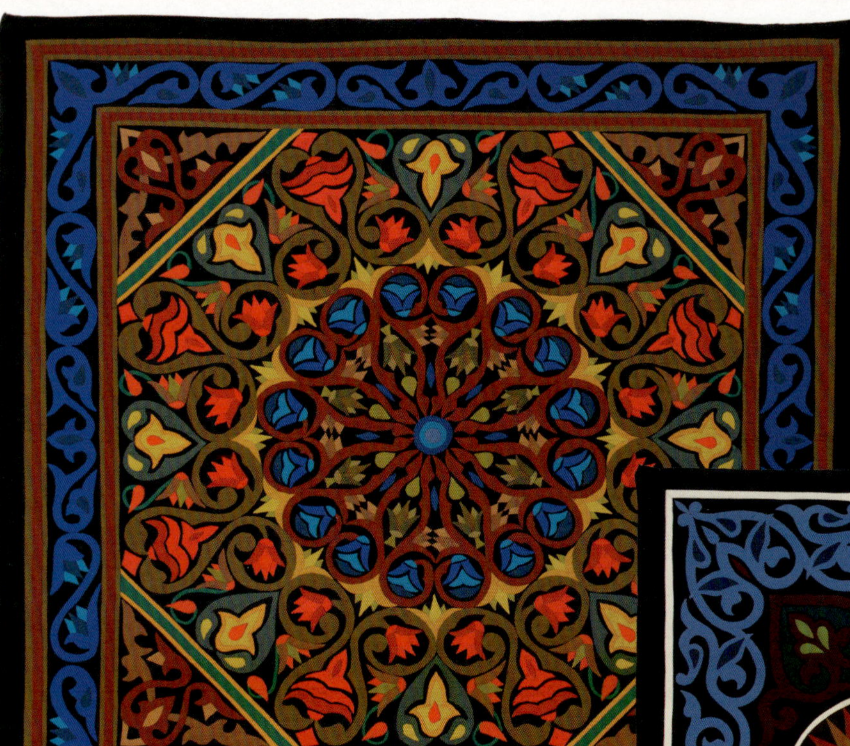

74 Hosam Al Farouk,
stitched by Motaz

Lotus with Romy and
border

Browns, greens, yellow,
and red with blue border

47" x 47"

75 Hosam Al Farouk,
stitched by Wael

Lotus columns Pharaonic

Browns, greens, gold, and
red with blue borders

59" x 69"

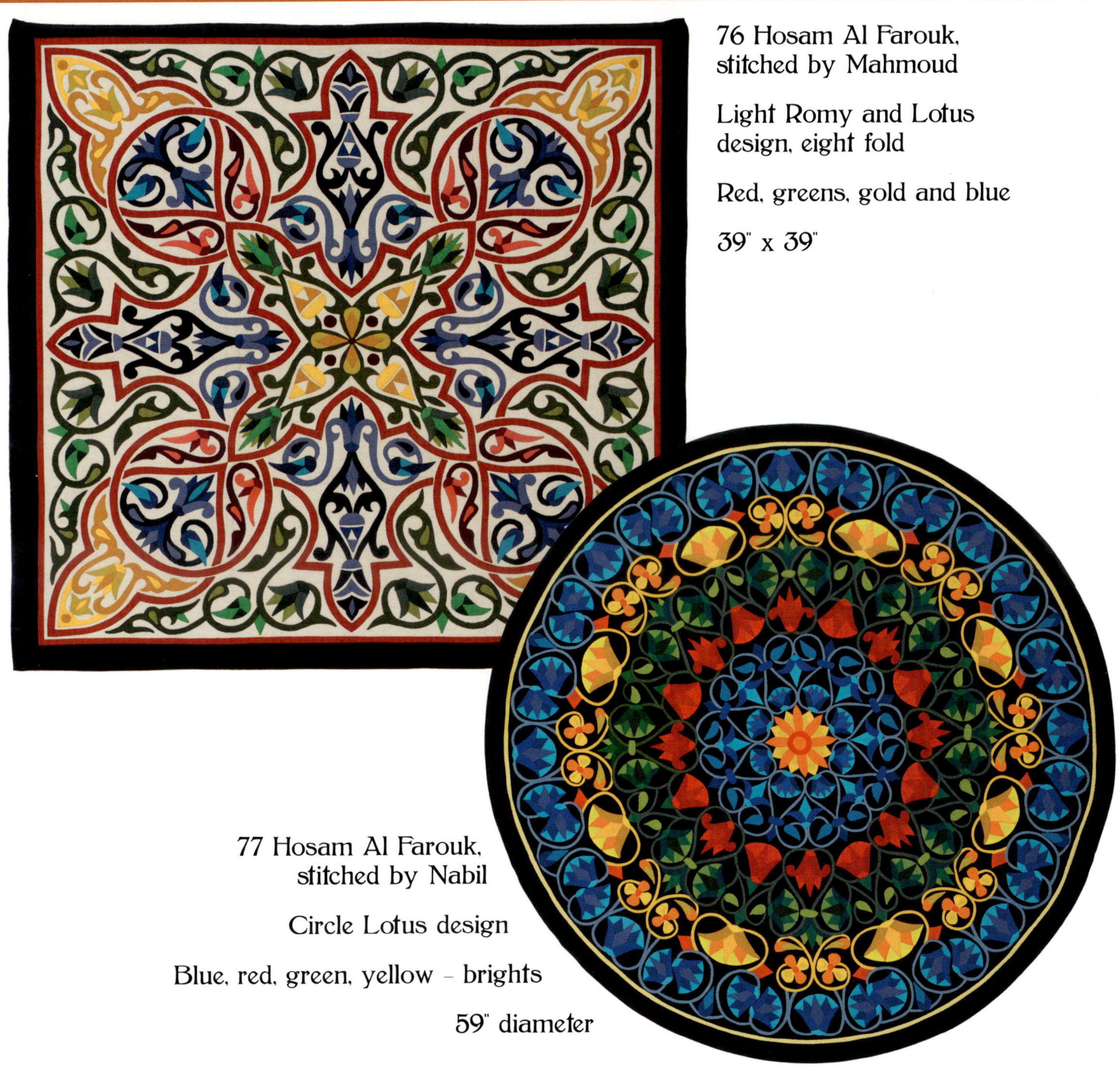

76 Hosam Al Farouk,
stitched by Mahmoud

Light Romy and Lotus
design, eight fold

Red, greens, gold and blue

39" x 39"

77 Hosam Al Farouk,
stitched by Nabil

Circle Lotus design

Blue, red, green, yellow – brights

59" diameter

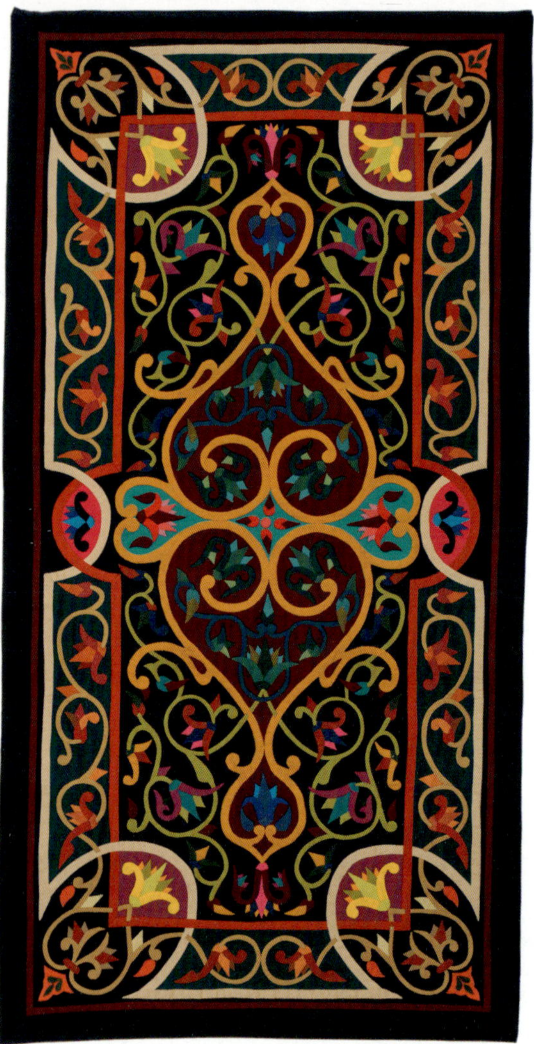

78 Hosam Al Farouk, stitched by Moksen

Long twin design Lotus with Romy

Green, burgundy, gold on navy with green border

39" x 78"

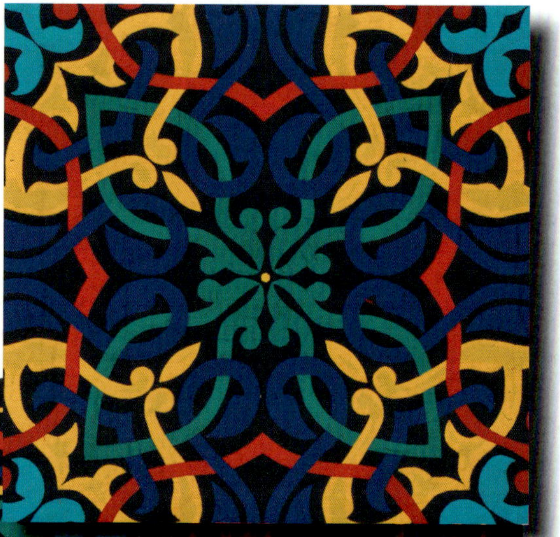

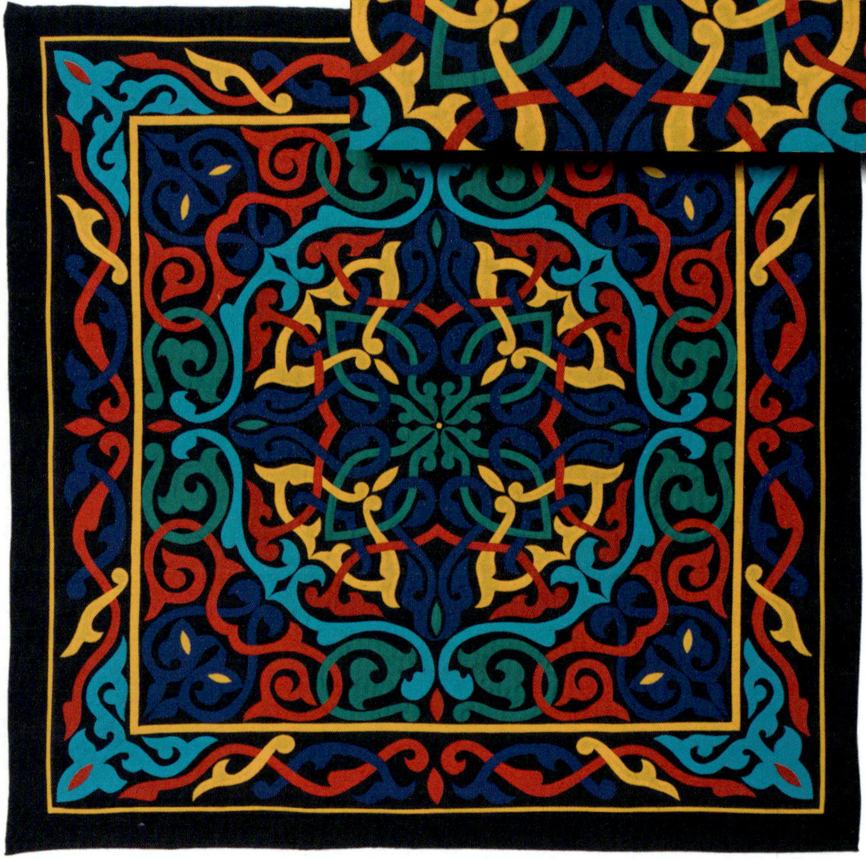

79 Hosam Al Farouk, stitched by Mohamed Ali

Square Romy design

Red, turquoise, blue, and yellow on dark

43" x 43"

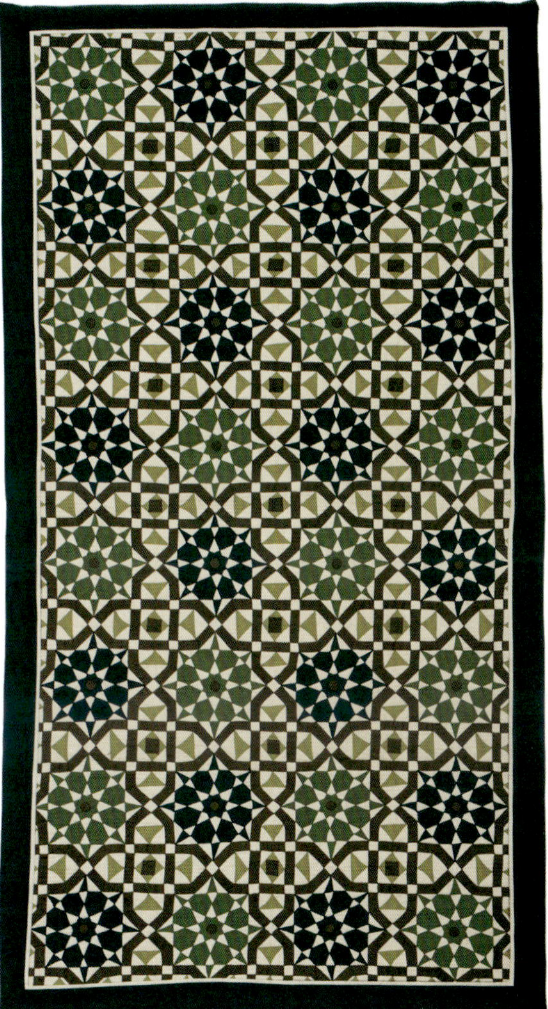

80 Hosam Al Farouk, stitched by Mahmoud

Arabesque

Zippered Floor Pillow Cover

Greens on cream

39" x 71"

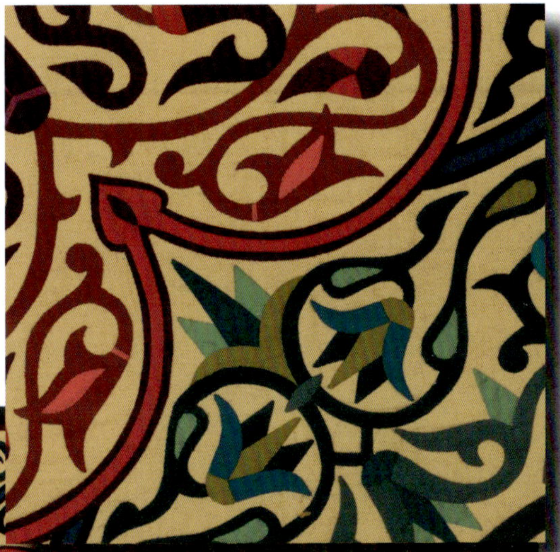

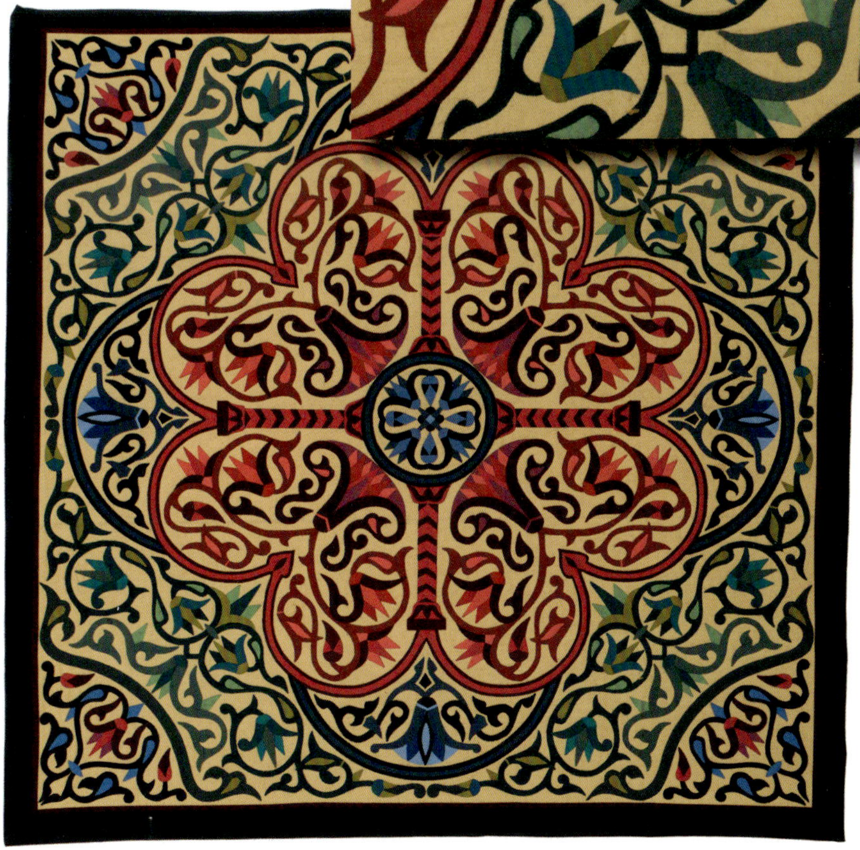

81 Hosam Al Farouk, stitched by Mohamed Ali

Lotus and cross–column design

Pink, green, and blue

55" x 55"

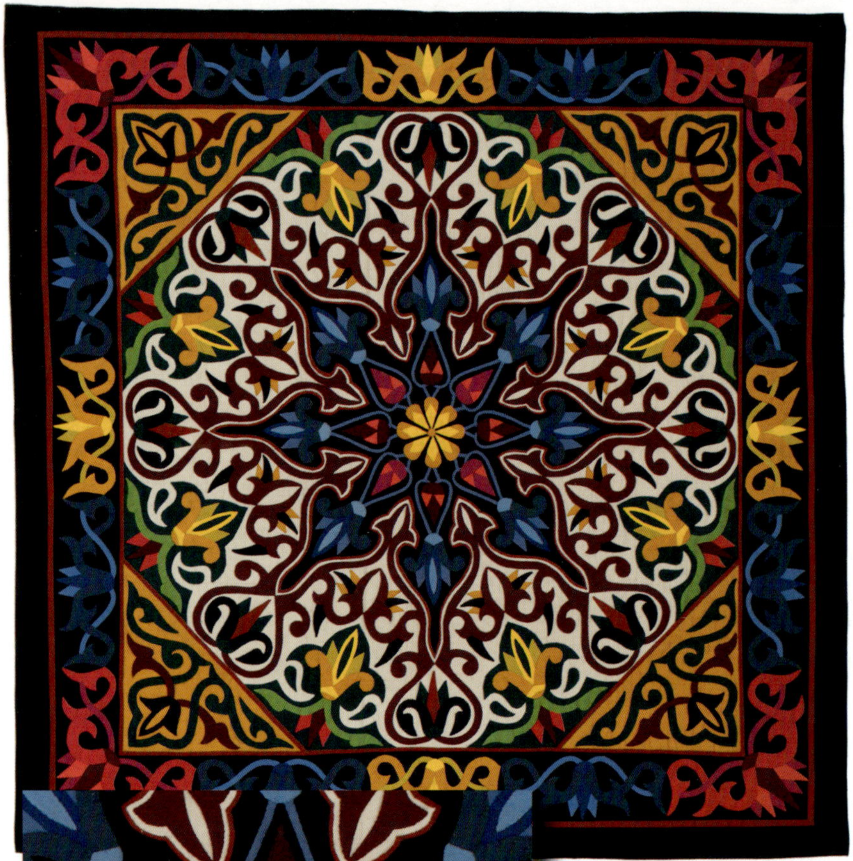

82 Hosam Al Farouk, stitched by Sameh

Lotus and Romy Star, 16–fold design

Blues and yellow on white

47" x 47"

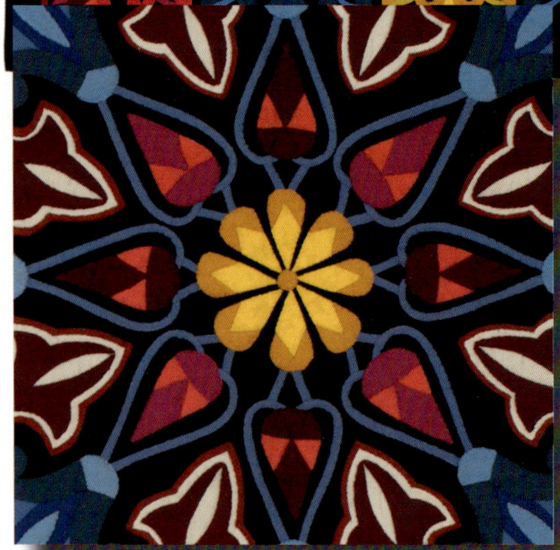

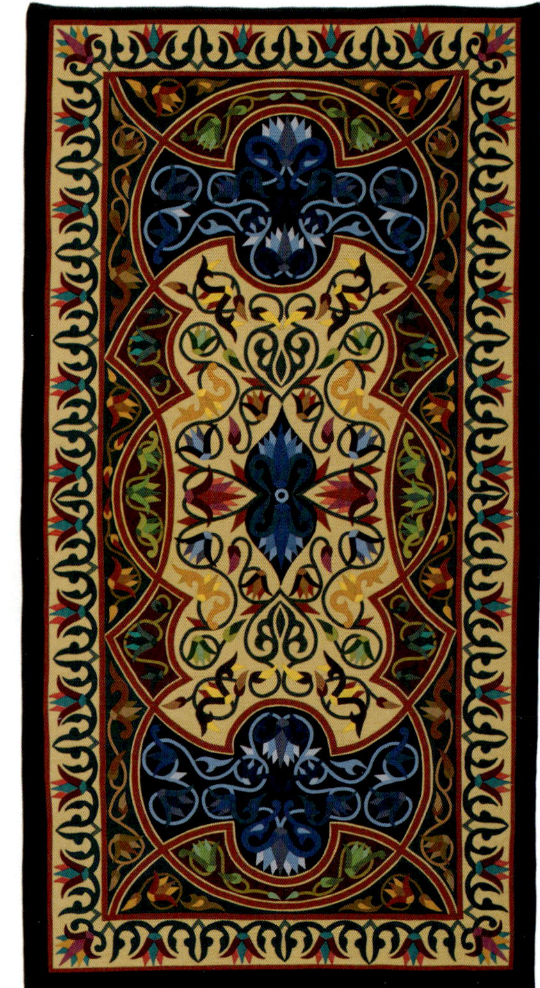

83 Hosam Al Farouk, stitched by Amr Mustafa

Long Lotus and Islamic design

Blues, reds, and greens on white with burgundy border

39" x 78"

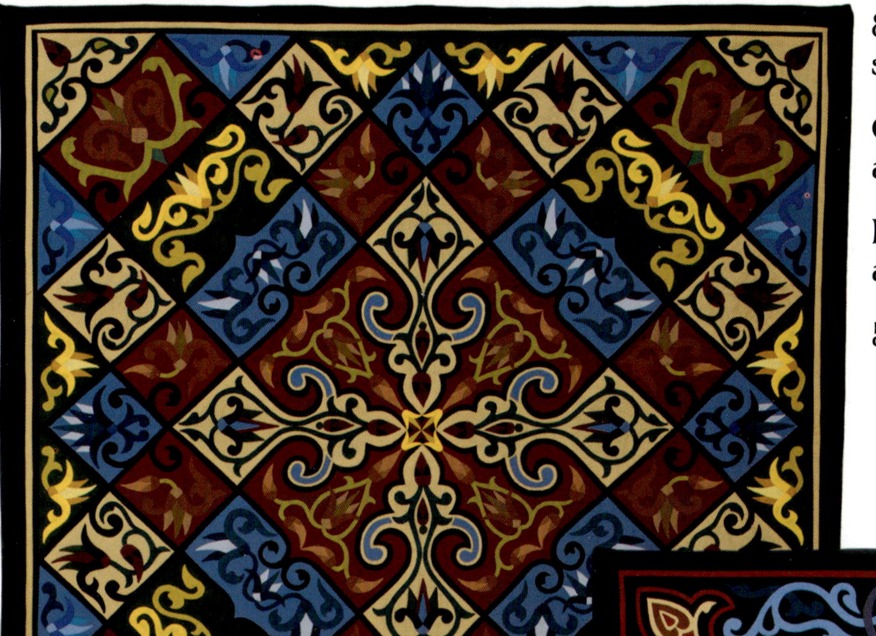

84 Hosam Al Farouk,
stitched by Amr Mustafa

Geometric squares
and Romy

Blues, reds, yellow,
and greens on black

55" x 55"

85 Hosam Al Farouk

Double cross with
Islamic patterning

Reds and blues on
cream and black

55" x 55"

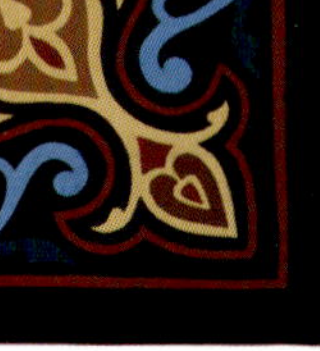

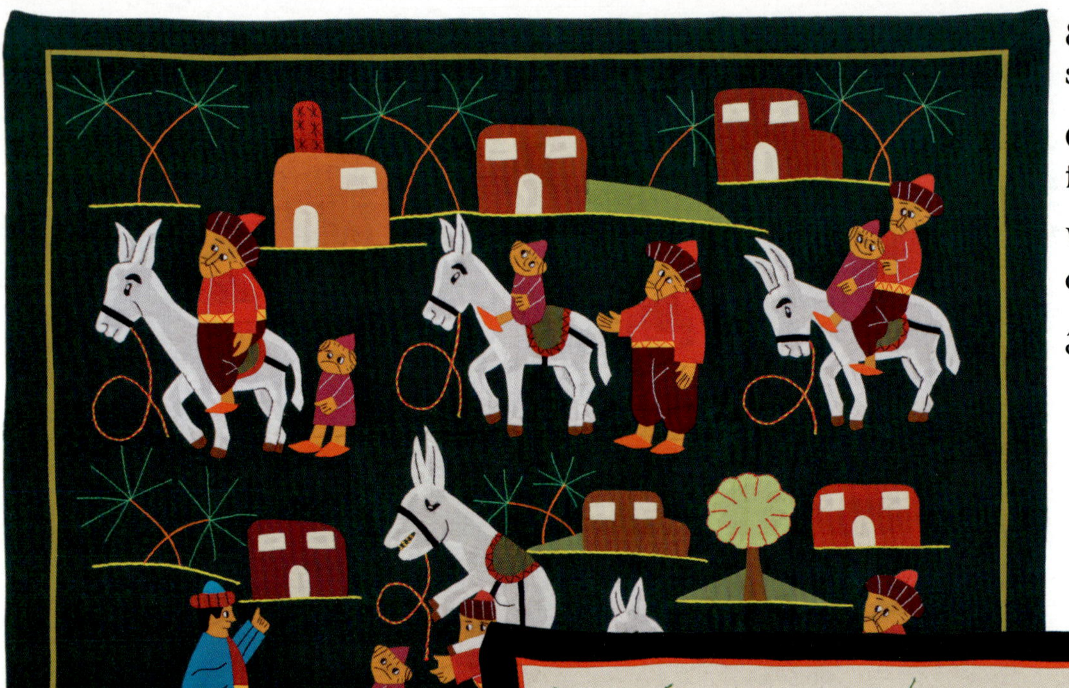

86 Hosam Al Farouk, stitched by Mohtaz

Goha and the Donkey – folk story

White and multicolors on green

39" x 41"

87 Hosam Al Farouk

Goha on cream canvas

Multicolors on cream

39" x 41"

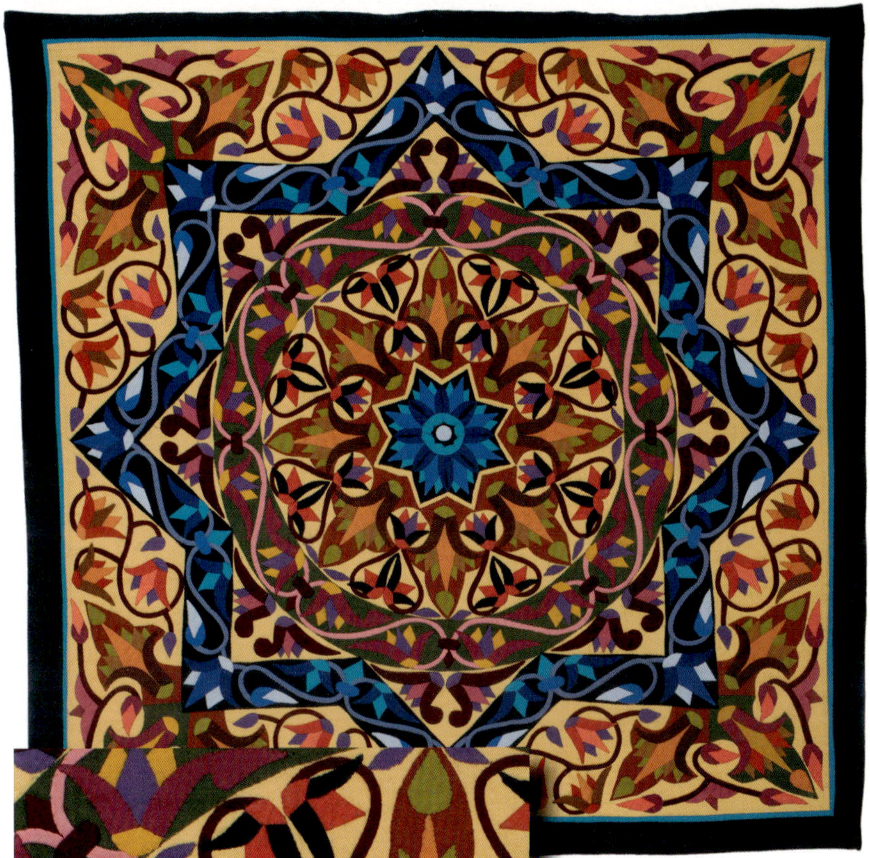

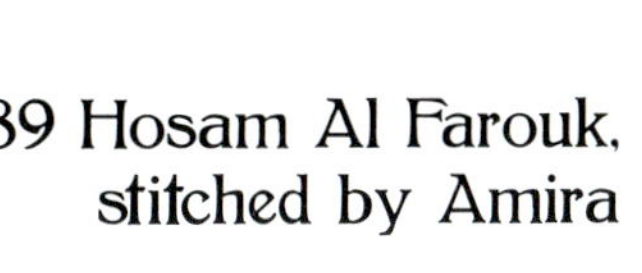

88 Hosam Al Farouk, stitched by
Wafa'a wife of Mohtaz

Lotus with blue Eight-Point Star –
16-fold Eight-Point Star design

Purples, green, browns, and
blues on cream

41" x 41"

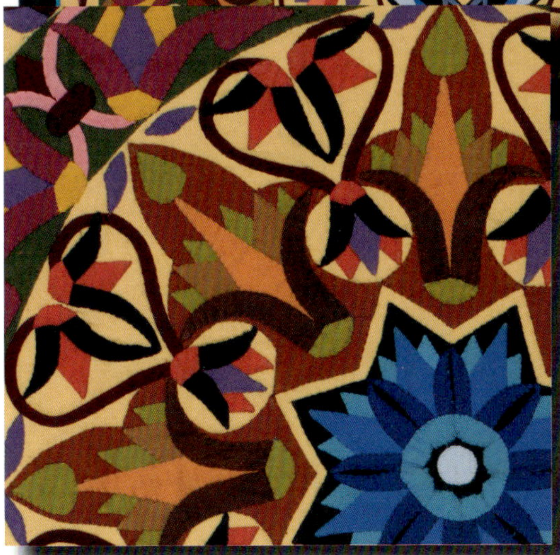

89 Hosam Al Farouk,
stitched by Amira

Lotus, long medallion
with Romy, border
and circles on corners

Burgundy, pink, and
red on beige with
dark border

39" x 78"

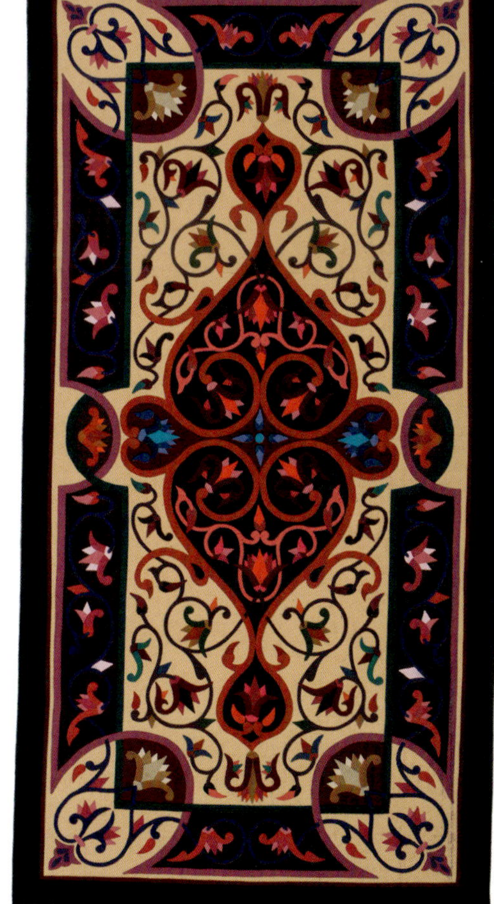

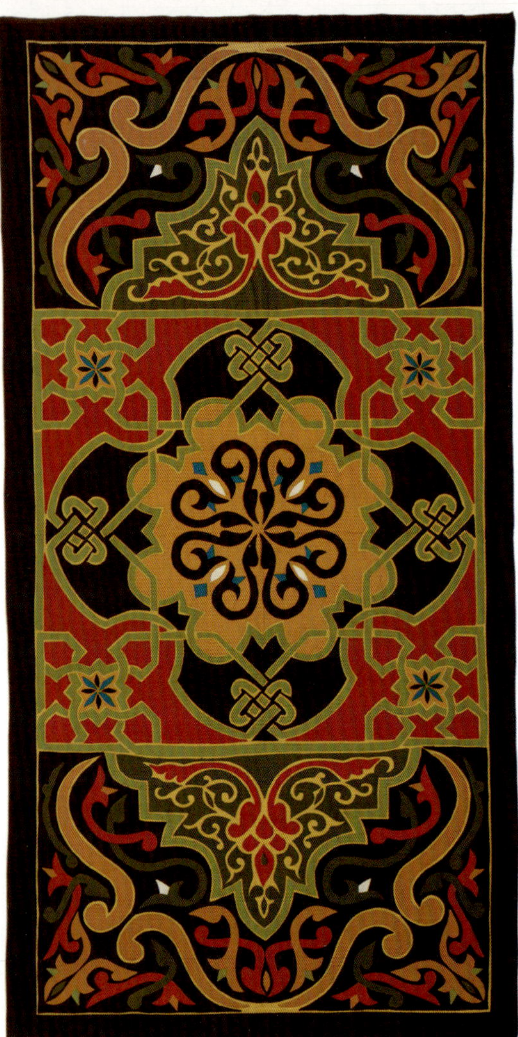

90 Ahmed Goma, stitched by Mohamed Kamal

Islamic and Romy design

Green and tan on brown and red

35" x 73"

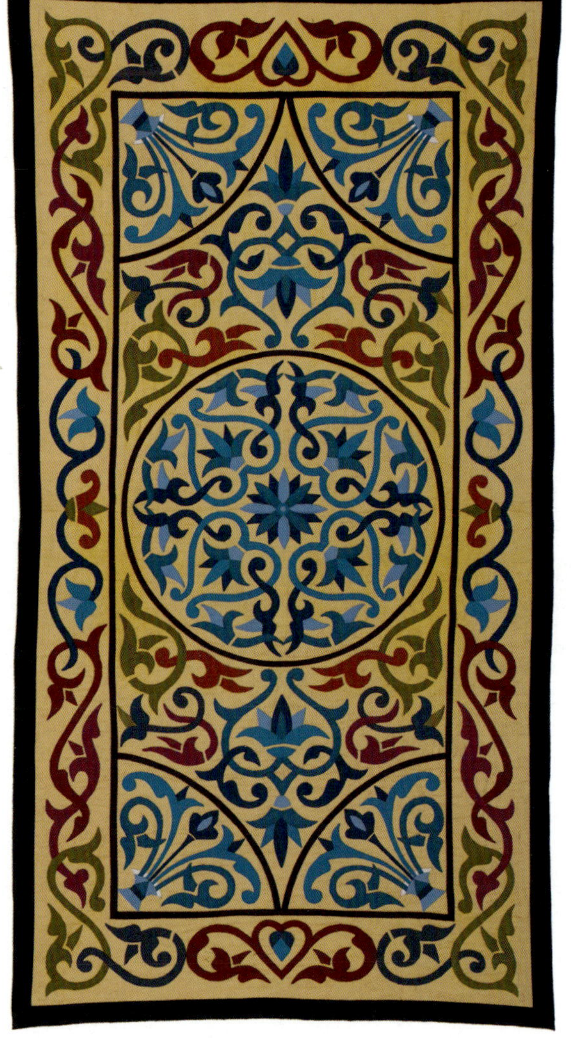

91 Ahmed Goma, stitched by Walid Hussein

Islamic door design, Romy border

Blues, greens, and reds on dark cream – light

35" x 71"

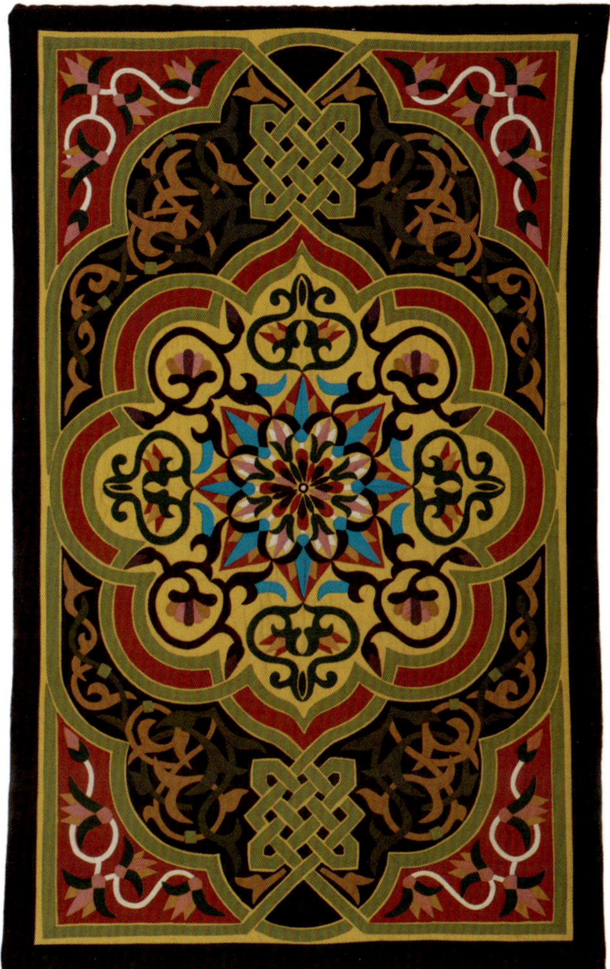

92 Ahmed Goma,
stitched by Amr

Islamic door design,
Romy border

Greens and reds on
3 backgrounds

39" x 64"

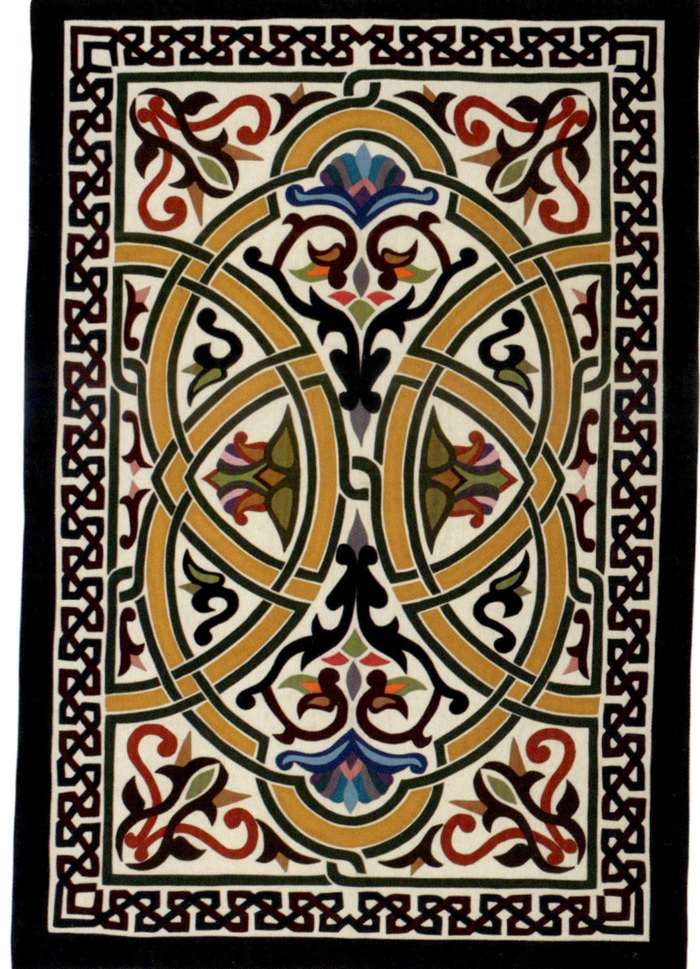

93 Ahmed Goma,
stitched by Amr

Islamic design

Mustard, blue, and
red on white

39" x 57"

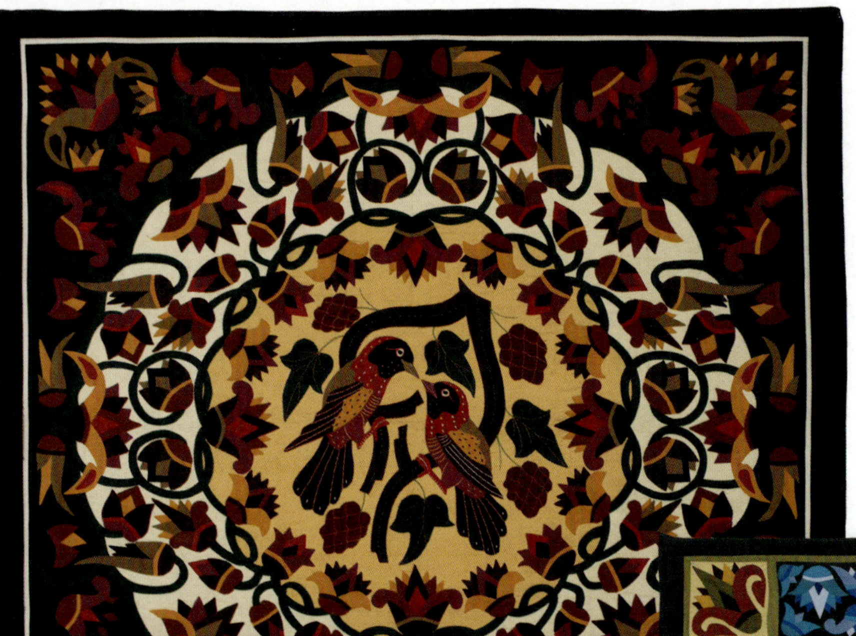

94 Tarek Fattoh,
stitched by Sameh

Birds in a circle
of Lotus

Greens and reds on
cream, dark border

43" x 43"

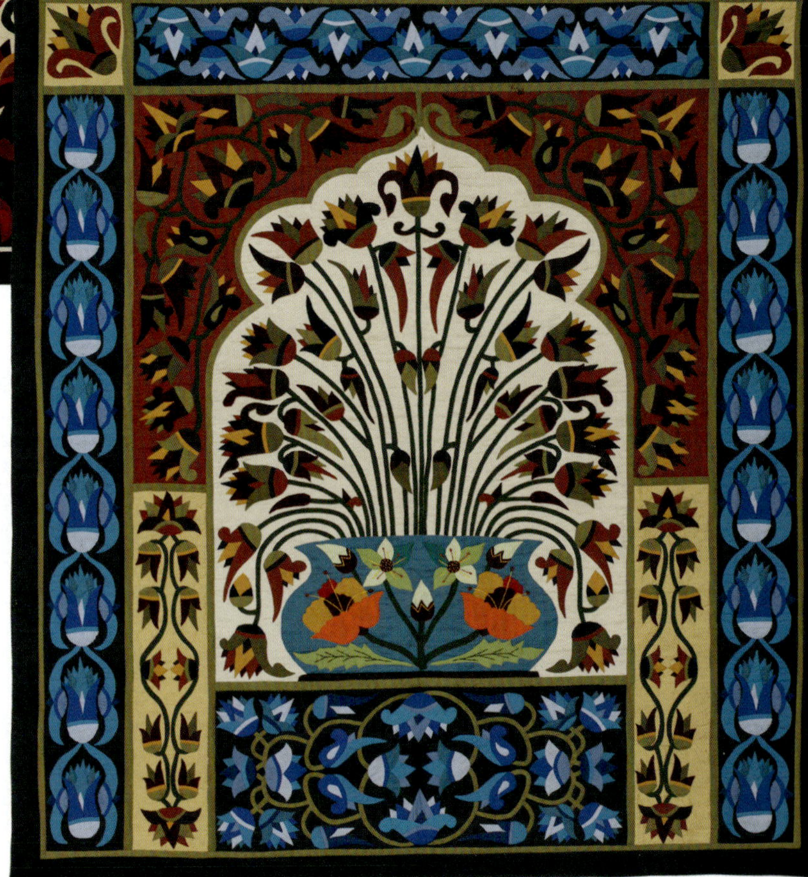

95 Mohamed Ibrahim,
stitched by Hamed Ibrahim

Lotus in a vase,
Lotus borders

Greens and reds on
red and cream, blue border

43" x 43"

Jenny Bowker
Curator of the Stitch Like An Egyption Exhibit

Jenny Bowker, textile artist, lived in Egypt for years while her husband was the Austrialian Ambassador. She created these quilts from photos she took in Egypt.

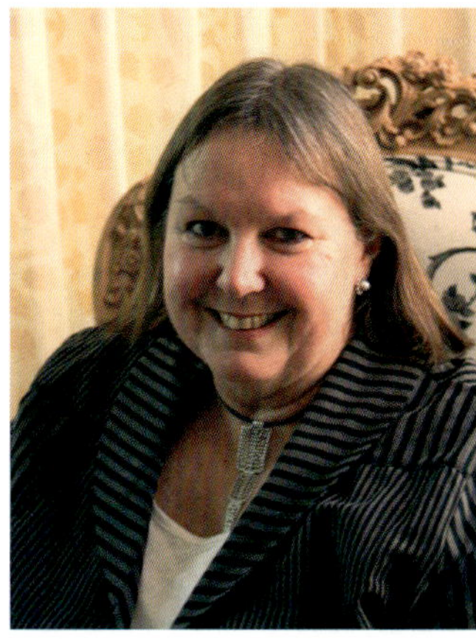

Photos by Jenny Bowker

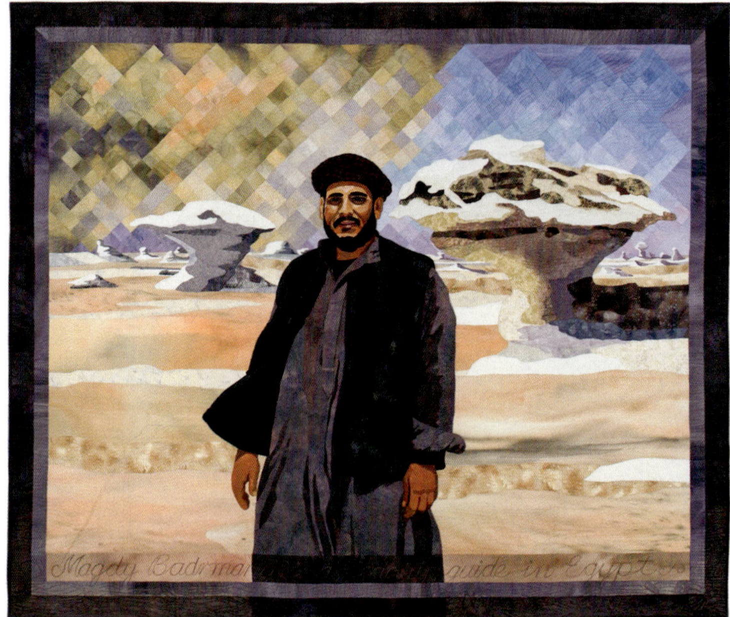

SAND STORM OVER THE WHITE DESERT, 82" x 97"
Magdy Badrmany is a Bedouin guide in the White Desert of Egypt and a very good friend. My family and friends often camped there with him. On one occasion I watched an incredible sandstorm building in the distance and swirling in. The desert changed colour - grey and yellow skies coloured by the sand changed the white chalk formations' colours to silver and lilac. Warmed by blue sky and sunshine, they were rich and creamy.

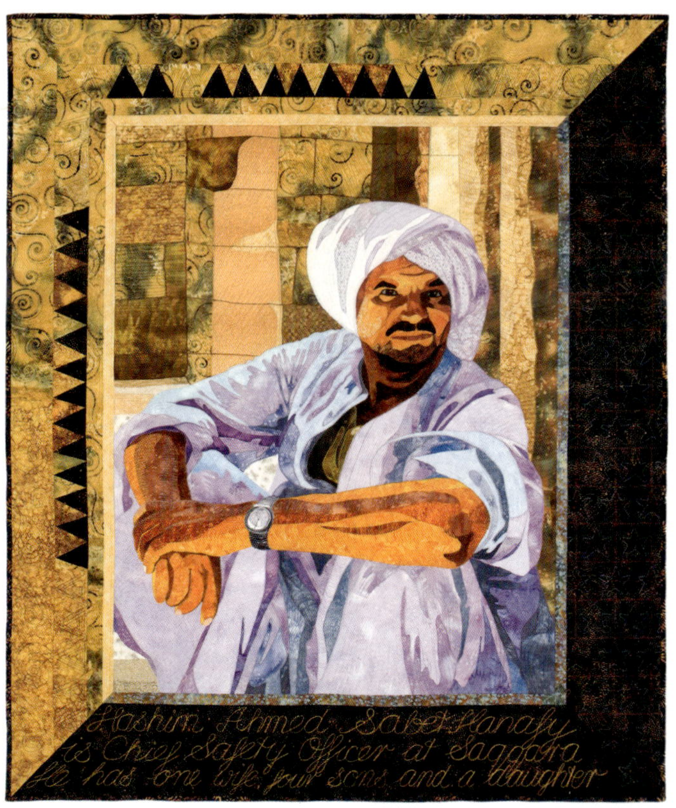

HASHIM, 58" x 71"
Hashim is a guard at the funerary complex of the Stepped Pyramid of Zoser (the first pyramid) at Saqqara in Egypt. On a blistering day I had sent my visitors into the sun after a briefing on what they would see, and settled into a breezeway in the long walkway through the 'papyrus' carved columns. Hashim kept me company and talked of his own contentment with his job, but for his son he has a dream of education and university and that he will be something better. He said, "Life is hard, in Egypt." It was a statement and not a complaint. I love the region. The thing I will remember most about Egypt is the stoic practicality of its people, and the kindness and generosity which has nothing to do with wealth.

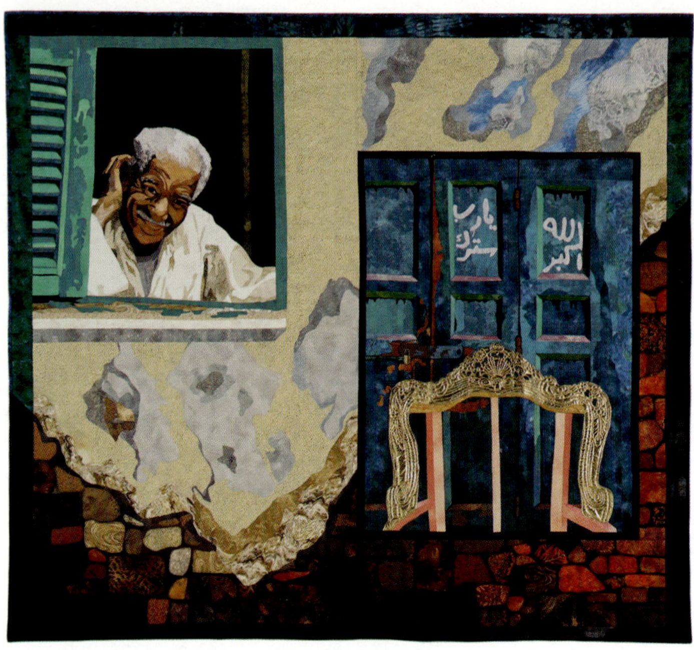

ABU ALI AND THE GILDED CHAIRS
87" x 79"

Abu Ali is usually strikingly dressed in black and white in the area where he carves chairs. He is guaranteed a living, as this is one thing even the wealthy Egyptians will spend money on. The chairs are gilded and covered in elaborate fabrics, silks and satins and flocked velvets. It is so strange to walk in the tiny overcrowded streets of the furniture areas and see, among the dirt, these chair frames glowing like jewels.

On this day I had arrived to bring him some photographs and found that he was not well. He was moved and thrilled to get the photos, and this is when I took this picture.

I began this series to let people look into the eyes of my hardworking Egyptian friends and to see that most Moslems are just like us.

Photos by Jenny Bowker

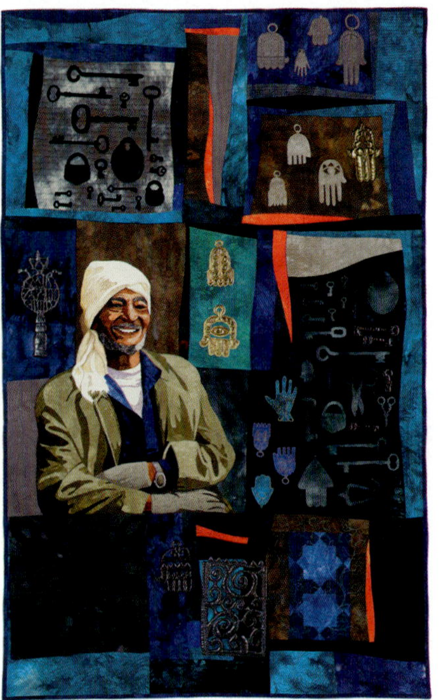

ITTAYER AND THE FRIDAY MARKET IN THE CITY OF THE DEAD
58" x 79"

Ittayer has a junk stall in the City of the Dead. It is not tidy – it is messy, dirty, and cluttered, but he occasionally has treasures. He has a wonderful welcoming smile. I have a collection of old keys, and a few locks, and hamzas - the hand-shaped protection against the Jealous Eye.

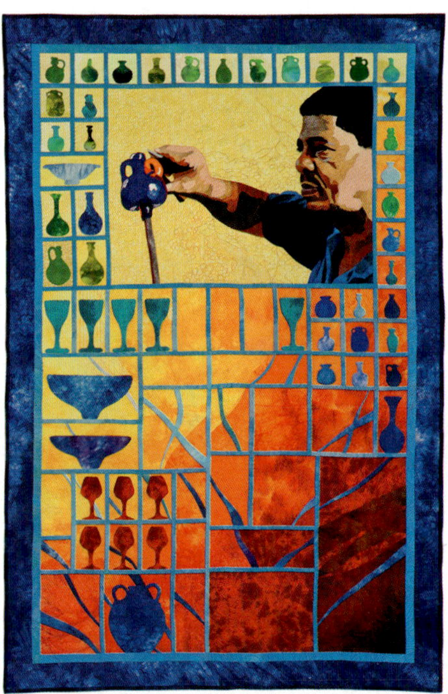

HASSAN AND THE GLASS
60" x 79"

Hassan blows glass in a tiny room in the centre of a square opposite Qaitbay Mosque in the City of the Dead in Cairo. The room is overwhelmingly hot, even in winter, and shelves around the room are packed with bright treasures. Colours are so vivid that they seem to trap the fire inside the glass.